Instructor's Manual
to accompany

STEPS TO WRITING WELL

or

STEPS TO WRITING WELL
WITH ADDITIONAL READINGS

Instructor's Manual
to accompany

STEPS TO WRITING WELL
Seventh Edition

or

STEPS TO WRITING WELL
WITH ADDITIONAL READINGS
Fourth Edition

Jean Wyrick

Prepared by
Anne Machin Norris

Harcourt Brace College Publishers

Fort Worth   Philadelphia   San Diego   New York   Orlando   Austin   San Antonio
Toronto   Montreal   London   Sydney   Tokyo

Cover Image: *Rouen Cathedral: Facade and Tour d'Albane (Morning effect), 1892–1894.* Oscar Claude Monet. Oil on canvas (41 3/4 x 29 1/8 in.). Tompkins Collection. Courtesy Museum of Fine Arts, Boston.

ISBN: 0-15-507240-4

Address for Orders
Harcourt Brace College Publishers, 6277 Sea Harbor Drive, Orlando, FL 32887-6777
1-800-782-4479

Address for Editorial Correspondence
Harcourt Brace College Publishers, 301 Commerce Street, Suite 3700, Fort Worth, TX 76102

Web Site Address
http://www.hbcollege.com

Printed in the United States of America

8 9 0 1 2 3 4 5 6 7   023   9 8 7 6 5 4 3 2 1

Harcourt Brace College Publishers

CONTENTS

SECTION ONE 1
    Suggested Teaching Tools to Use with *Steps to Writing Well* 3
    Suggestions for Effective Essay Assignments 7
    A Few Notes on Portfolio Grading 10
    A Sample Course Plan 12

SECTION TWO 21
    Part One   The Basics of the Short Story 23
        Chapter 1 Prewriting 23
        Chapter 2 The Thesis Statement 27
        Chapter 3 The Body Paragraphs 31
        Chapter 4 Beginnings and Endings 37
        Chapter 5 Drafting and Revising: Creative Thinking, Critical Thinking 39
        Chapter 6 Effective Sentences 43
        Chapter 7 Word Logic 49
        Chapter 8 The Reading-Writing Connection 55
    Part Two   Purposes, Modes, and Strategies 57
        Chapter 9 Exposition 57
        Chapter 10 Argumentation 75
        Chapter 11 Description 81
        Chapter 12 Narration 85
        Chapter 13 Writing Essays Using Multiple Strategies 89
    Part Three   Special Assignments 93
        Chapter 14 Writing a Paper Using Research 93
        Chapter 15 Writing about Literature 97
        Chapter 16 Writing In-Class Assignments 99
    Part Four   A Concise Handbook 101
        Chapter 17 Major Errors in Grammar 101
        Chapter 18 A Concise Guide to Punctuation 107
        Chapter 19 A Concise Guide to Mechanics 113

SECTION THREE 115
    Part Five   Additional Readings 117
        Chapter 20 Exposition: Development by Example 117
        Chapter 21 Exposition: Process Analysis 125
        Chapter 22 Exposition: Comparison/Contrast 131
        Chapter 23 Exposition: Definition 139
        Chapter 24 Exposition: Division/Classification 145
        Chapter 25 Exposition: Causal Analysis 151
        Chapter 26 Argumentation 159
        Chapter 27 Description 167
        Chapter 28 Narration 175
        Chapter 29 Essays for Further Analysis: Multiple Strategies and Styles 181
        Chapter 30 Literature 191

PREFACE

As Jean Wyrick notes in "To the Teacher" in *Steps to Writing Well,* the seventh edition of the text offers accessible, informal, practical advice to student writers. *Steps'* style and format encourage interaction between the student reader and the text: discussions of writing strategies are crisp and straightforward; numerous student and professional essays offer opportunities for critique and analysis; practice exercises, with a fine dose of humor, allow a self-check of concepts studied; the handbook section of the text is a quick, efficient resource.

This instructor's manual is also designed to be a practical, hands-on reference for composition teachers. It describes some possible teaching tools to use with *Steps* and offers suggestions for effective assignments as well as a sample course plan. These sections of the manual are an overview of only some of the many possible teaching strategies and course arrangements that can be used with *Steps.* Answers to all practice exercises in *Steps* are also included.

ACKNOWLEDGMENTS

Many thanks to Anne Norris for her excellent contributions to the "Additional Reading" section of the sixth edition of this instructor's manual, and a very special thanks to Jean Wyrick for her tremendous support and advice.

Instructor's Manual
to accompany

STEPS TO WRITING WELL

or

STEPS TO WRITING WELL
WITH ADDITIONAL READINGS

SECTION ONE

SUGGESTED TEACHING TOOLS TO USE WITH
STEPS TO WRITING WELL

The composition maxim, "The only way to learn to write is by writing and rewriting" is underscored in *Steps* as a premium is placed on writing and revision through creative and critical thinking (Chapter 5). Keeping journals (Chapter 1) and participating in collaborative activities (Chapter 5) are two ways instructors might encourage students to examine their own writing process and analyze the writing of others, enabling them to bring new insights to their own work.

THE JOURNAL
Chapter 1 of *Steps to Writing Well* discusses the benefits of keeping a journal and offers students suggested uses for the journal. Jean Wyrick notes that there are numerous advantages in requiring a journal:

Benefits for the student:
—encourages thinking, learning, discovery
—helps sequence the students' writing processes
—provides practice of skills
—improves the quality of the written product
—reduces writing anxiety
—improves class participation

Benefits for the teacher:
—provides opportunities to intervene in the students' composing stages
—ensures better "products" to evaluate
—may replace traditional assignments
—may reduce grading time and pressure
—discourages "passive" reading of assigned material
—allows the monitoring of class progress, understanding of material

For journals to be an effective part of a college composition course, expectations for journal assignments should be clearly communicated to the students. The journal provides them with a chance to write informally, perhaps experimenting with their writing and taking more risks than they would in a traditional, formal essay assignment. This is not to say, however, that journals are not to be taken seriously by student writers: if journals are to be a success, with assignments that are rewarding for the instructor as well as the students, there should be accountability. When students are thoroughly invested in their journals, a great deal of learning can take place, but if the journal is not incorporated into class discussion and reviewed periodically by the instructor, the journal's effectiveness is likely to be diminished. Here is a sample description of a journal from one composition teacher's course guide:

> In much the same way that an artist uses a sketchbook to record ideas and preliminary sketches for larger works, your journal is a tool for you to document your ideas and progress in the writing field over the course of the semester. Assignments for the journal will be varied and will take place

both in and out of class. A couple of notes: be sure to title and date each assignment, doing them in the order they are assigned. In addition to written assignments, class notes should also be recorded in the journal. In short, your journal should be a complete record of your preliminary writings for each essay. A suggestion: consider reserving the last few pages of your journal to record assignments for each class meeting.

STRUCTURE

Please organize your journal by unit, labeling the first section "Introduction." As we complete each unit and move on to the next, title each section according to the writing strategy currently being explored ("Narration," "Description," etc.).

GRADING

Journals will be collected at the conclusion of each unit, often the last class before an essay is due, and will be returned the following class period. Each assignment will be noted as complete or incomplete, with credit given for each thoroughly completed assignment. At the end of the term, your journal grade will be determined as a percentage (# completed out of the # possible) and converted to a letter grade.

When giving take-home journal assignments, detailed instructions help guarantee completed, thorough journal entries. Here is a sample assignment:

JOURNAL ASSIGNMENT THREE

For most of this course, we have been discussing the importance of writing clear, straightforward essays that communicate directly to the reader. These were characterized by unity, coherence, a clear, narrow focus, effective paragraph development, and creative introductions and conclusions.

For this journal assignment, choose a *cover story* from any *Time* or *Newsweek* magazine. Then do the following:

—Copy it on a copy machine and staple it to this assignment sheet. Make sure the entire article is included.

—Use a pen or pencil to mark up the essay (unmarked essays are not acceptable). Make note of things like transitional devices, thesis statements, interesting concrete language, paragraph development, etc. In other words, try to notice as many of the things we talked about in class as possible.

—In the margin or somewhere near each mark, identify what it is you are marking.

—On a separate sheet of paper, write four or five sentences evaluating the essay, making some comment about the audience for which the essay is intended, the transitional devices used, and in general how you would evaluate the overall quality of the writing, based, again, on the things we have been discussing in class.

COLLABORATIVE ACTIVITIES

In Chapter 5 of *Steps to Writing Well*, students are given advice on maximizing the effectiveness of revision workshops. There are also guidelines for the composition instructor to ensure successful collaborative activities. Jean Wyrick offers the following advice.

SUGGESTIONS FOR ORGANIZING COLLABORATIVE ACTIVITIES

Small-group work and peer revision workshops sometimes aren't as productive as we'd like them to be. Here are some suggestions for organizing collaborative activities that you might find useful.

1. Hand out a sample student paper the class session before the workshop. Ask students, at home, to write a brief summary and to make a note of the paper's major strengths and weaknesses. Ask them to bring this paper, their notes, and their own drafts to class.

2. Hand out written instructions for the workshop or write them on the board before class. At the top of the sheet/board include a statement of your (realistic, limited) goals for this activity.

3. Discuss your goals with the class. Talk about the value of giving and taking constructive criticism. (What kinds of comments are most helpful, which aren't, etc.) Go over the instructions for the workshop *before* they move into pairs or groups.

4. Clearly state in writing an "accountability factor." Students must always know they are responsible for producing something that will be shared with the entire class at the end of the activity—a report, something to be written on the board, a reading of a revision, something.

5. State the time limit for this activity. (Lie. Tell them less time than you really can allow for this activity.) Fifteen to twenty minutes on one activity is probably tops. Always leave yourself maximum time to discuss the results of the activity. Whole-class discussion time should always be as long as (or longer than) the group time.

6. Always design the groups and match up students for pair-work. Avoid matching buddies. Keep track of who is working with whom from week to week.

7. If you're doing small-group work, assign jobs: a recorder to keep notes, a time-keeper to move folks along, a reporter to present results, a facilitator to lead discussion, a "devil's advocate" to introduce a different point of view, and so on. Make each member of the group responsible for something.

8. Discuss the instructions for the workshop. If you're running a revision workshop, the instructions should be a limited number of clearly defined, specific tasks. Too many tasks addressing every aspect of the paper do not produce good results!

9. A note on the nature of the tasks: avoid simple yes/no questions (Is this paragraph adequately developed? "Yup."). It is frequently easier for students who are insecure about their ability to critique to offer advice after they have described what they see. Example: Underline the main thought of this paragraph. Number the specific examples (pieces of evidence, whatever) that support this idea. Would the paragraph profit from additional support? Why or why not? If yes, where?

10. Model the tasks on the sample student essay that you handed out last class. Modeling the responses shows students what you expect and also builds confidence in their ability to address these tasks, to critique a peer's paper.

11. Allow students to add at least one question to the list of tasks. They may do this as a class, or if they're in pairs, each student may add one individually. (As the semester progresses, the class should gradually take over the list of tasks.)

12. Circulate as they work. Move quietly from group to group. Listen, ask questions, but try not to assume leadership of the group. Note any common problems you might want to address at the end of the activity. Announce the time; give nearing-the-end warnings when appropriate ("Ten minutes left—you should have finished the first three tasks by this time").

13. Put the class back together as a whole and call for the results from some of the groups/pairs. Discuss the results and then demand that students apply wisdom gleaned from the activity to their own papers. Actual hands-on revision is best, but oral responses are good if you're short on time.

14. Always allow students to have the last word on the activity. Why was/wasn't it helpful? How could it be improved next time? These make good journal questions, especially if students want to complain about a partner who wasn't giving useful feedback.

15. When the papers are revised, let the peer-editor have a read before the papers come in. A quickie read-and-pass is also fun—interesting, too, how the papers get better when students know many of their peers will be reading them.

16. Have many, many workshops on a paper, not just one huge one toward the end. Vary the kinds of questions/tasks: reader-based, criterion-based, descriptive, evaluative, and so on. Fit the workshops to the stage of the writing process—one on purpose and audience, one on organization and development, one on mechanics—whatever fits your purpose, your students and the assignment.

17. After you've read through the papers, consider "publishing" some of the better efforts by duplicating them for the class or by using an overhead projector or by reading them aloud. You don't always have to reprint an entire essay—you can

also present the class with a list of effective sentences, phrases, images, or even "A+" action verbs that were direct hits!

Here is a sample assignment sheet for a small-group activity focusing on the argumentative essay "Students, Take Note!" (Chapter 10):

"Students, Take Note!": A Group Perspective

Instructions: As a group, discuss and answer each of the following questions. Choose a recorder to jot down group decisions, a facilitator to lead your group's discussion, a timekeeper (you'll have 15 minutes for this activity), and a reporter to present your findings to the class.

1) Consider the author's thesis. What evidence does the author give to support his or her claim? Why is(n't) this evidence effective? Where is the author most convincing? Least convincing?

2) Does the author acknowledge/refute opposition to his or her claim? Why is(n't) this effective? What are some arguments against the author's claim that the essay does not acknowledge?

3) Are there any logical fallacies in the essay? If so, identify them.

4) Your group's assessment of the overall effectiveness of the essay:

SUGGESTIONS FOR EFFECTIVE ESSAY ASSIGNMENTS

As student writers, we all either heard about or experienced firsthand the horror of the instructor who assigned papers with a vague verbal statement of topic, length, and due date. The students in this case are left with a bewildering array of questions. How should the paper be developed? Is research required? How formal should the presentation be? These unanswered questions often lead to confusion and writer's block, resulting in a last-minute "shot in the dark" paper that does not accurately reflect the student's writing ability. In short, vague assignments often yield unsuccessful essays; thorough assignments encourage clear and effective student responses. To revise a well-known phrase, "As composition teachers sow, so shall they reap."

While classroom discussions, activities, and *Steps to Writing Well* will provide students with thorough guidelines for approaching a variety of writing strategies and styles, an effective essay assignment is vital to ensuring that student writers are able to transfer what they have learned in class and from the text to their own writing. Instructor's expectations for major essay assignments should be clearly established, preferably in a printed handout that students can refer to throughout their writing process.

Here is a sample assignment sheet for an argumentative essay requiring research:

Argumentative Essay Assignment

Argumentative skills are a part of everyday life: on a daily basis, each of us makes claims about issues large or small. Consider the argumentative elements of issues that you're concerned about. To make this assignment a meaningful and successful endeavor, choose a topic of *narrow* scope so you can successfully support your stance. Consider, the following guideline for your selection: *avoid* global issues and claims that are supported more by emotion or faith than fact. The key to a successful argumentative essay is to *combine cold, hard facts with logic to form a convincing argument.*

Once you've selected a topic, examine the subject for a debatable claim. If the claim is arguable (is there an opposing side?) you have the focus for an argumentative essay. To clarify your purpose and goals for writing this essay, it is vital to define a specific audience.

Argumentative essays must be fully *supported* with a combination of personal perspective and research. This is a research paper: in addition to personal knowledge you must use the following support for your claim:

> 1) a minimum of 5 written sources to provide current, relevant support for your paper. Attach a photocopy of all sources to rough draft.

> 2) an interview with an authority on the subject

Essay Length: 4-7 pages, plus Works Cited page

Due Dates

> Topic proposal presentation/review: Tues. 4/14 and Thurs. 4/16

> Completed rough draft due for take-home peer review: Tues. 4/28

> In-class workshop on rough draft: Thurs. 4/30

> Final draft: Tues. 5/5

For particularly demanding assignments, a follow-up "suggestion" sheet, guiding writers away from pitfalls the instructor has often seen in student essays, is sometimes helpful as students work to select a topic:

GUIDELINES FOR SELECTING
A SUCCESSFUL ARGUMENTATIVE ESSAY TOPIC

> 1) Is the topic narrowed enough to be successfully and convincingly developed in a 4–7 page essay? A very specific topic, well presented, is more effective than a broad (if seemingly more significant) topic that can't be developed fully.

> 2) Is there a legitimate opposition?

> 3) Can you refute the opposition's argument?

> 4) Can your position be argued and supported primarily with fact and logic rather than emotion, faith, or a morality-based stance?

> 5) Is it an issue you have experience with or have a vested interest in? To be convincing, your voice must be heard.

Topics to Avoid

1) Issues that have been argued into the ground for years (e.g., capital punishment, the drinking age, the voting age) unless you have a new angle on an old topic.

2) Issues that you feel so passionately about that you can't argue your position logically (rather than emotionally) or acknowledge arguments of the opposition.

After students have selected a topic and have begun drafting, a detailed reminder of essay criteria can be a valuable resource. A criteria sheet like the following sample not only provides student writers with a self-assessment tool, it can also be used in peer workshops as a tool for reviewing the writing of others. Finally, the instructor can use this same sheet as a grading guideline.

Argumentative Essay Criteria Sheet

I. FOCUS

Clearly stated? _____

Appropriate for scope of essay? _____

Established as arguable topic? _____

II. SUPPORT FOR CLAIM

Each statement of opinion/assertion
supported convincingly? _____

A logical rather than emotional base for argument? _____

Avoidance of logical fallacies? _____

Convincing support of overall claim? _____

Acknowledgment/refutation of opposition's claim? _____

III. USE OF SOURCES

Use of required research sources? _____

Effective use of sources as support? _____

Context/introduction of authority? _____

IV. STRUCTURE

Logical, coherent structure? _____

V. MLA CITATION FORMAT

Correct format for in-text citations? _____

Sources acknowledged appropriately? _____

Correct Works Cited format? _____

VI. MECHANICS

Free of mechanical errors? _____

VII.   AUDIENCE

Strong sense of audience/purpose?   _____

VIII.   OTHER CONSIDERATIONS

Appropriate title?   _____

Effective lead-in?   _____

Clear transitions?   _____

Meaningful conclusion?   _____

Overall maintenance of

focus/coherence/unity and development?   _____

A FEW NOTES ON PORTFOLIO GRADING

Many times an instructor looks at a student paper and thinks something like, "If Mary just had one more shot at this assignment, she'd have it," or "With some additional evidence, this would be a darned good argument!" How many times, after a week or more of rest from a project, has Mary been able to look at what she's written and then make similar comments about her own work?

Because of the typical structure of a composition class, however, teacher and student too often have to settle for what can be accomplished in a given time frame. To combat these somewhat arbitrary and frustrating limitations, instructors now sometimes turn to portfolio grading, or more appropriately, portfolio *writing*. In a portfolio class, students write and revise assignments continuously throughout the term and submit a final collection of their essays for a course grade. The obvious idea is that students can achieve better results with the benefit of time and perspective to help them revise. In this way, then, portfolio grading is one way to match class structure more closely to current *process* writing theory. Students can be evaluated on their cumulative efforts, on their overall assimilation of class concepts, and on their revising ability.

Portfolio writing can be integrated into class structure in a variety of ways. A student's grade might depend, for instance, on one final review of his or her portfolio with no grades given on any writing to that point. Comments on drafts might include general strengths and weaknesses or notes regarding specific mechanical issues you are working on in class, but no score is suggested. Students are encouraged by this system to focus more on their process than just on the outcome. Instead of meeting an artificial deadline established only by the syllabus and a teacher's needs to space assignments efficiently throughout the term, students can try an unlimited number of drafts, different versions, new approaches, until they are satisfied with the result.

Another option is to collect and review student portfolios periodically, giving a grade for progress and quality at each review. Some teachers use a mid-term and a final portfolio, concentrating the grade to between 60 - 75% on the final collection to maintain the emphasis on revision. Others choose to review portfolios three times during the term, once for progress, once for a preliminary grade determination, and once for final analysis.

Still other instructors employ a configuration that combines traditional grading with the portfolio concept. You might, for example, collect essays and give grades as usual, making sure to make comments directed toward the student's pending revision. Then students can rework these graded essays throughout the term for inclusion in their final portfolio which will be reviewed for a final cumulative grade and averaged with their other term grades similarly to a final exam.

Whatever method is employed, successful instructors mold the style of portfolio writing to their own strengths and teaching styles as well as to their particular situations. The teacher with 100 students per term, a martyr indeed, cannot possibly do traditional grading and then tack on an additional element of portfolio grading if he or she intends to maintain any level of sanity. On the other hand, a teacher with one composition class might want to try using a number of individual conferences throughout the term, one or two preliminary portfolio reviews, and a culminating final portfolio. Assess your techniques and teaching conditions carefully and honestly, then design a configuration appropriate to those constraints.

When introducing a portfolio system, keep the following potential pitfalls in mind.

1. *Avoid grading your own work.* Too often, through well-meaning comments and directions, a teacher can appropriate a student's paper. Looking at too many drafts and making too many detailed comments makes the student dependent and stifles independent critical thinking. The student is then writing to achieve the teacher's vision of the paper, not his or her own. If a final portfolio reflects the teacher's expertise rather than the student's, the system is not working well. Questions ("What experience can you share to support this point?") and reader response comments ("At this point, I wasn't sure how these two paragraphs related") can be the most helpful in guiding students and avoiding this problem.

2. *Avoid grading **another** student's work.* As in any composition classroom, the portfolio class offers many opportunities for a student to get inappropriate help from others. A certain amount of in-class writing, of individual conferencing, and of requiring and checking multiple drafts will help minimize this problem.

3. *Expect and learn to manage student grade anxiety.* Students may worry greatly if their final evaluation will be satisfactory when they are not receiving periodic grades. On the other hand, some students may have an inflated idea of the quality of their work if they do not receive some early evaluation. Providing some method of early progress/quality assessment will help them understand where they stand in relationship to your standards. Such a preliminary assessment can be anything from an informal conference ending in a joint teacher/student determination of a grade and suggestions for improvement (a grade which is not recorded since every item is subject to revision) to a formal teacher-generated score which counts toward the term grade.

4. *Avoid increasing your work load.* While portfolio grading is not a way to cut back those lengthy hours of reading student work, it need not add to your hours either. The important thing to remember is that when you are looking at multiple drafts, you need not make as many comments on each. Pointing out one paragraph that needs a topic sentence, for example, and suggesting others can benefit from the same revision, helps the student review essays independently; and such instruction may lead to improved learning since the student is not dependent on your comments. Highlighting one or two comma splices and suggesting the student look for other mistakes of this kind can have the same result. Also, since the student is going to go back and rework these papers, you need not comment on issues you have not yet addressed in class. You can concentrate on single issues on each draft, a practice that will make both your job and the student's job more targeted and effective, less fragmented and frustrating.

5. *Avoid procrastination.* Some students might be inclined to hand in less carefully done work on early drafts when they know only the final product "counts." If you allow this to happen, you are either doing the student's revision work by reading and commenting or wasting your efforts before he or she has really put enough thinking or writing into the project. To avoid this problem, many instructors give appropriate credit for early drafts, encouraging students to present their best work at each stage.

Teacher procrastination is another possibility. Although the temptation might be to wait to look at papers carefully until the end of the term, only spot-checking early drafts, the quality of the final portfolios will be directly related to early and continuous guidance. Lengthy review and comments on the final collection might be interesting to some students, but will not be particularly instructive and will keep you working until the last minute before grades are due. One of the best ways to assign a final grade to the portfolio is to schedule individual conferences (these can be done in 15 - 20 minutes) in which the student reviews the portfolio with you and, together, you assess improvements, remaining weaknesses, and overall quality of the pieces in the collection, taking time to point out particularly strong revisions you have noted in several of the essays.

Implemented thoughtfully and individually, portfolio writing/grading can be very rewarding. For students, it can be a step toward more intrinsic motivation and greater independence as writers. For the instructor, it is a way to reflect a more realistic notion of the way good writing *really* happens—through a continual process of revision—and the portfolio can provide a better opportunity to observe and acknowledge substantive change in students' skills and habits.

A SAMPLE COURSE PLAN

Steps to Writing Well can be used with a wide variety of teaching styles and composition course structures. John Huxhold, professor of English at St. Louis Community College at Meramec, offers the following first-person account of teaching methods he uses with *Steps.* The seventh edition of *Steps* includes new chapters that are not included in Professor Huxhold's course plan. Instructors might assign Chapter 8, ("The Reading-Writing Connection,") early in the term to emphasize the vital relationship between critical, close reading and effective writing. Chapter 13, ("Putting It All Together: Writing an Essay Using Multiple Strategies") can be used to guide a culminating project emphasizing the skill of selecting appropriate strategies to match specific tasks and needs. To help students learn to analyze and respond to writing, Chapter 15 ("Writing an Essay About Literature") might be assigned after students have practiced several different strategies; such writing will help them with assignments across the curriculum.

INTRODUCTION TO THE COURSE

I like to subtitle my first meetings with students "Where Have We Been and How Did We End Up Here?" We need to know some things about each other, not only the rules of the class, the schedule of assignments, and our expectations of each other, but especially the kind of attitudes and cultural biases we have as we approach the task of writing. We talk a lot about the effects of television—how it lowers attention span, makes us less interested in discussing things in any but the most superficial terms *(CNN Headline News),* and leads to passivity.

The most important part of our discussion, however, centers on the fact that writing is an analytical activity whereas watching television is primarily a synthetic one. I point out that we are rapidly becoming a culture that gets bits and pieces of information that are not necessarily in a logical order and we are required to synthesize that information in a way that makes sense to us. Not only have we gotten very good at this (adults predicted that kids would not understand *Sesame Street* because the segments were not logically ordered like, say, *Mr. Rogers' Neighborhood,* but of course the kids picked up the sense of things without skipping a beat), but we have come to prefer this way of dealing with our environment. For example, we like discussion classes where we create the learning environment rather than lectures where it is created for us.

The upshot is that we begin our composition course with some very strong synthetic biases:

We are in a hurry. Since the average time a single, stationary image stays on a television screen is only 5 seconds, the average commercial is 30 seconds or less, and the average television show is only 30 minutes, we have become impatient with activities that don't move along. We drive over the speed limit, we try to get a parking spot close to the door, and we try to get into the shortest checkout line because even a wait of only 10 minutes is intolerable.

We want every experience to be sensuous. Television is very good at using images that not only come at us at a rapid pace but also incorporate more than just one sense. Not only is the face attractively posed and shaped (sight), but also the soda can presses on the lips in an extreme close-up (touch), the carbonation fizzes against a musical background while the model murmurs how delicious the soda is (sound), and the tongue rolling around the lips makes it seem like you could almost (taste) the soda. And that is just taking a sip of soda! No wonder, then, that the interior of even a modestly priced car has surround-stereo, bucket seats, and carpeting, and that in your suburban bathroom you can watch television from your sunken tub or get a snack from the little fridge nearby.

We are impatient with connections. Television images flit back and forth between rooms, continents, and galaxies in a split second. A television image is only concerned only with the end of the journey, not with the means for getting there. On *Bewitched* and *Star Trek* people get beamed somewhere with the flick of a finger or a switch; the manner in which that occurs is, well, magic! Getting there is none of the fun—it's being there that counts.

The impact of all of this on writing is that it takes a long time to walk from the parking lot to class, leaving behind our bucket seats and stereo sound and entering an analytical environment where the room is rather plain and quiet, the desks are not conducive to passivity, and the teacher talks for almost an hour. We now make telephone calls rather than write letters, and watching television has virtually replaced recreational reading. All of this directly affects the kinds of writing errors and problems that pop up later in the course—problems like having difficulty choosing topics, the lack of connection (transition) between sentences and paragraphs, and a tendency to cover a topic superficially.

This is when I assign "To the Student" in *Steps* where the sections on "Finding the Right Attitude" and "Why Write?" take on more significance after our discussion of the effects of television. I finish these first class sessions by reminding students of the importance of audience and voice, and we go through that section in *Steps*.

Their first paper assignment is virtually open-ended. They are to write as much as they can on the subject of television. By now they have plenty of information, and the more they write, the better their grade, as long as what they write is reasonably clear and intelligent. Since there are so few "requirements," their fear of writing rarely surfaces, they get their first experience with a step-by-step analytical process that takes time and concentration, and they discover that writing is not only a way to communicate but a way to learn and discover as well.

CHAPTER 11: DESCRIPTION
Doing Chapter 11 now has two advantages. Students at this point are looking around for something to write about, and describing something from their immediate experience is not only easy but natural for them. We work on sensitizing their sensory apparatus by looking at all the details of a four-inch-square piece of sod and making lists of details for all the senses, not just sight. It is also a good time to begin hammering home the idea that specific, concrete adjectives, verbs, and nouns are the essence of good writing. I have students revise a sentence like "The person went out

of the building, went to the vehicle, and drove away" to make it more vivid and pal-pable and at the same time to create a dominant impression.

CHAPTER 1: PREWRITING
Finding a subject is always a problem. When I assign a topic, everyone complains that they can't write about it; when I let them choose, they don't know what to do. Along with the following suggestions in the chapter, I have them do a dialogue with them-selves about what other classes they are taking, what information interests them in those classes, what they do in their spare time, what makes them happy, what makes them angry. When they come to my office for help, we go through the same dialogue, but they tend to trust me more than themselves at first about what constitutes a good topic.

CHAPTER 2: THE THESIS STATEMENT
Focusing on the thesis statement comes naturally after choosing a topic, and even if they didn't think so beforehand, everybody comes to realize that a paper needs to have its intention stated clearly. The idea of an essay map, however, comes less auto-matically. Students want to jump into the body of the paper without further ado. This section is concluded with my pointing out that unity, coherence, and emphasis throughout a paper are very important, and we practice in class with essays that we make up on the spot. At this point, students draft an essay (this will be a very early draft) in which they develop one idea they have focused during the study of Chapters 1 and 2.

CHAPTER 3: THE BODY PARAGRAPHS
Perhaps the most telling aspect of a sophisticated paper is the way its paragraphs are developed. I begin with a series of overheads that not only goes step-by-step from a sim-ple topic sentence (with a subject and an attitude) to a fully developed paragraph but also has a long exercise about using specific, concrete language. I relate the sections on paragraph unity and coherence to our discussion of overall unity, coherence, and empha-sis, and I also assign a section on writing with examples found in Chapter 9.

CHAPTER 4: BEGINNINGS AND ENDINGS

CHAPTER 5: DRAFTING AND REVISING: CREATIVE THINKING, CRITICAL THINKING
The paper assignment associated with this chapter is essentially an extensive rewrite of the previous paper written during the study of Chapter 2. The subject must be rethought and perhaps given a sharper focus, the introduction must use one or more of the techniques we discussed while studying Chapter 4, the conclusion must be something other than a summary and should incorporate the features of a good con-clusion outlined in Chapter 4, and the body paragraphs must show more coherent, sophisticated development. Chapter 5 gives students even more suggestions about the revision process.

CHAPTER 9: EXPOSITION

CLASSIFICATION, COMPARISON/CONTRAST, DEFINITION

By now we are more than halfway through the course. Since our discussions of the body paragraphs were conducted in rather fine detail, the next three papers are a nice change of pace—they open up to a more general framework, while at the same time reinforcing previously introduced material. For example, the formats for classification and comparison/contrast essays are not that difficult to understand or to execute. The real problem is to make them worth reading. In the comparison/contrast essay, I lay out the format (block or point by point) using a cat and a dog. The points are fur, feet, tail, and ears. Once the format is clear, I ask students why the paper would still be a failure, and we then discover that by giving the paper a purpose and more substance (contrasting the two animals in order to choose a pet), the audience becomes a big consideration, and the points are altered to suit the new focus of the subject.

The classification and comparison/contrast experiences are good preparation for the definition essay. Students now have at their disposal these as well as description strategies that will help them carry out the suggestions in the "Definition" section of the chapter. Subject matter and audience are also (again) important considerations.

CHAPTER 6: EFFECTIVE SENTENCES

CHAPTER 7: WORD LOGIC

At this point, a pause in the course allows for scheduled conferences with individual students to discuss their work so far. Before they come in, however, we have several class sessions focused on Chapters 6 and 7. Students break up into small groups, show their papers to each other, and examine each other's sentences and word logic. Then each student comes to me and together we make up a one-page list describing each writer's strengths and weaknesses, with an emphasis on those things presented in the two chapters.

CHAPTER 9: EXPOSITION

CAUSAL ANALYSIS

I use causal analysis as the basis for the final paper of the semester. I expect it to be the students' longest, best effort, the culmination of all the knowledge and skills we have been developing through fifteen weeks. At various points in the text, a brief definition might be required, a description might make an idea more vivid, or a contrast between two points of view could show why an event happened. In any case students are to bring all of their resources as writers to bear on this paper.

CHAPTER 10: ARGUMENTATION

TEACHING ARGUMENTATION AND RESEARCH

The essays that precede argumentation and research, whether earlier in the semester or in an earlier course, are very personal and subjective. Whether or not I agree with the writer or find the topic convincing is subordinate to making sure that the topic is expressed clearly and directly. With argumentation and research, however, things get more objective. It is no longer sufficient for a student to have an opinion and express it clearly; now that opinion must be supported with logical arguments and substantive research in which outside sources are called in to make the student's case stronger.

Argument and research can, of course, be integrated into personal essays; after all, every essay with a thesis statement (or topic sentence, for that matter) expresses both a point of view on a subject and an attitude; it is, in fact, an argument. Contrasting a cat and a dog, for example, to demonstrate that a cat would make a better pet is taking a stand on an issue that could have been resolved in another way by another writer. Furthermore, the use of sources to document one or more points in a personal essay is certainly effective.

In many curricula, however, argumentation and the research paper are separate from personal essays. But whether integrated or not, the most critical factor in the success of either one in the classroom is continually to make the connection to the students' individual, real experience. Nothing is more deadly than an argument or a research paper written in isolation from a student's curriculum, career, or life at home.

ARGUMENTATION

Teaching argumentation before doing research activities works well because writing arguments is an excellent link between the personal essay and the research paper. For one thing, all the way back when students were talking about lead-ins and conclusions, it was stressed that a writer needs to keep the audience clearly in mind. It comes up here again in the form of questions like "Who is this trying to persuade?" or "Why would someone with a closed mind want to hear my side?" or, perhaps most important, "How can I get this person to listen?" Also, virtually the entire argumentative essay is an "introduction" because in every paragraph the writer needs to be keenly aware of not only informing the reader but persuading the reader as well.

Another reason argument is a good link between the personal essay and the research paper is that most of the principles and techniques of argumentation can be drawn from the students' own experience without their having to learn special research techniques or confront the task of finding and documenting research materials. Writing persuasively is an intermediate level of support between the informative subjectivity of the personal essay and the relatively more objective format of the full-blown research paper. The patterns of organization mentioned in the chapter are also a link to familiar territory that was traversed in earlier personal essays.

Furthermore, a wealth of supplementary material is available for discussing argument in the form of the ubiquitous television commercial. The commercial is an argument in miniature and uses not just the usual formal argumentative techniques but some formidable persuasive ones as well. Also, the argumentative techniques and fallacies are easy for students to spot in the blatantly bad examples. I don't spend much time pinpointing the difference between argument and persuasion except to note that persuasion has the more negative connotation. Nevertheless, I like my students to be good at both, and both can be done responsibly.

The "Common Logical Fallacies" section mentions virtually all logic problems that come up in any discussion of argumentative techniques. Rather than have students memorize the list and then go hunting for examples, I like to make up arguments in class using subjects taken from contemporary events. I purposely play devil's advocate to get students interested (and sometimes angry), and then ask them to describe what I was doing, and finally show them that this problem in argumentation has a name. For example, I will begin a class by mentioning that on the way to school I heard a song by a particular rock group and that while it was pretty good, most of the guys in the band are, after all, probably on drugs and look pretty disgusting, so I would never buy one of their albums. It doesn't take long for students to recognize the *ad hominem* argument, even though they may not call it that. Written assignments are easy to develop, once students realize, as the chapter introduction points out, that argument is all around them. One of the most successful exercises is to have students write letters to the editor of local newspapers (including neighborhood papers) or even to national publications like *USA Today* or *Time*. A large proportion of the letters sent in get published, and the thrill of seeing their name in print is a great incentive for amateur writers.

Longer papers are more successful if the subject is close to the writer. Arguing for allowing AIDS victims a normal place in the workforce is merely an abstract exercise if the writer, an only child with a widowed mother, goes to school full time and lives at home. And how many papers we could get on legalizing marijuana that repeat the same old abstract clichés! On the other hand, if a student chooses to argue about the ethics and long-term effectiveness of downsizing from his or her own perspective after being laid off, then a ring of authenticity will pervade the paper.

CHAPTER 13: WRITING A PAPER USING RESEARCH
Before plunging into the research paper project, it is a good idea to spend some time in a discussion similar to the "Why Write?" portion in the "To the Student" section of the introduction to the text. You might point out the following:

Other classes will require research. At some time during their college experience, most students will have to do some form of documented research. In classes other than English composition, the teacher will usually be concentrating on the finished paper, not helping very much in the process of writing it. Directions from the teacher for such papers will vary from a rather detailed outline of the subject and focus of the essay to a simple statement like "Have a twelve-page paper finished in three weeks, pick the subject yourself, and make sure the format and documentation are correct." One legitimate function of the research paper experience in an English class, therefore, is to give students the capability of writing for other classes without the trauma of spending most of their energies scrambling to learn the process.

Research skills are used all the time. Living as we do in a democracy and a consumer society, we make decisions every day that can be made more intelligently if we research the subject, as well as critically examine the arguments used to put forward ideas. Which senatorial candidate to choose might best be decided on the basis of research into the candidates' voting records in the state legislature; the purchase of a new hair dryer may have been influenced by an article in *Consumer Reports* which reflected the results of the magazine's research; a couple may decide to deliver their baby by means of natural childbirth based on a medical study citing the many advantages of this method; a complaint about food in the college cafeteria might be documented with a survey and some recommendations for change presented in an article in the school newspaper; highly paid product managers direct expensive marketing research before launching a new product. Skill in finding and evaluating sources of information is an important part of being an informed and successful citizen. Discussions related to this point also develop the attitude in students that they need more information not only to persuade others but to convince themselves as well.

Knowing where to look and what to look for saves time. Perhaps the most obvious benefit of the research paper experience is getting acquainted with libraries. In my classes, one of my main goals as students tackle research is to make them comfortable with the way libraries are organized and with what resources are available to them. After finishing my class, they are equipped to handle virtually any library of any size since they know what the ground rules are. I would even say that the library experience is more important to students than is the final grade on the research paper. Depending on how much time you have, you might want to give your classes a one-hour tour of the library (or have a library staff member do it for you) and point out to students all of the many reference works and bibliographies that most of them never knew existed and that are invaluable in finding information efficiently. What I am trying to dispel is the attitude that the library is a daunting maze of arcane information—that the chance of finding something besides the *Reader's Guide to Periodical Literature* is remote, even impossible.

Don't, however, overlook other kinds of resources off campus. Community and consumer organizations, as well as cultural institutions like local and state historical societies, are excellent places to get the sort of documentation the subject of the paper requires.

The paper is a concrete, practical experience. Nothing is worse than writing, or reading, a paper which is written only to fulfill an assignment. The writer needs to show enthusiasm for the subject, consider the audience, and demonstrate a genuine interest in engaging and persuading the reader—in short, the process for finding good topics for research papers is identical to that for shorter papers mentioned at the beginning of *Steps*. One added consideration, however, is that a student needs to evaluate how many and what sorts of resources are available—it would be tough to write a substantive essay on some aspect of the *Star Wars* movies if the library has a meager collection of books and periodicals about film.

Furthermore, at some schools, the research paper is devoted exclusively to library topics. ("It's the last chance we have at them!") If you have the option, however, I have had more success guiding students through a paper they are writing for another class. Even better are methods that two of my colleagues used in their classes. One has her students research their careers. She requires them to go to our Career Information Center, interview people working in the students' career area at local businesses, and do research in the library on both the career areas (job prospects, working conditions) and several companies devoted to that product or service. Another teacher in my department has students survey local cultural institutions to see what their needs are and then produce a project (not necessarily a formal paper) that fills that need. For example, Elsah, Illinois, is a small town on the Mississippi (near St. Louis) that is a historical landmark. The town needed a slide-tape presentation for its museum, so students did research about the town (including interviews with older residents), took pictures, and finally wrote a 15-page script that coordinated the slides into a 20-minute presentation. In addition to researching, the students were constantly using the editing and revision skills they learned while writing personal essays. The enthusiasm these students display for their work is only one of the many benefits of this approach. It also transforms the teacher from a sadistic taskmaster into a resource, a person who will help students achieve good results.

SECTION TWO

PART ONE

THE BASICS OF THE SHORT STORY

CHAPTER 1: PREWRITING

P. 3

SUMMARY

GETTING STARTED
—you have some valuable ideas to tell your reader
—you want to communicate those ideas to your reader

SELECTING A SUBJECT
—start early
—select something in which you currently have a strong interest
—narrow a large subject

FINDING YOUR ESSAY'S PURPOSE AND FOCUS
—listing
—freewriting
—looping
—the boomerang
—clustering
—cubing
—interviewing
—the cross-examination
—sketching
—dramatizing the subject

AFTER YOU'VE FOUND YOUR FOCUS
Practice, p. 19

DISCOVER YOUR AUDIENCE

HOW TO IDENTIFY YOUR READERS
    —check to see if it is a specific or a general audience.
    —if the audience is specific, why would they want to read your essay?
    —what knowledge does the audience have of your subject?
    —what attitudes and emotional states does the audience have?
    —what sets the audience apart from any other?
Readers don't like to be bored.
Readers hate confusion and disorder.
Readers want to think and learn.
Readers want to see what you see, feel what you feel.
Readers are turned off by writers with pretentious, phony voices.

Practice, p. 25

KEEPING A JOURNAL
    —helps you conquer the blank page
    —improves your powers of observation
    —saves your brilliant ideas
    —saves other people's brilliant ideas
    —allows you to be creative
    —prepares you for class
    —records responses to class discussions
    —focuses on a problem
    —practices audience awareness
    —describes your own writing process
    —records a progress report -makes you sensitive to language
    —enables you to write your own textbook

ANSWERS TO "PRACTICE" EXERCISES

Practice, p. 19

A. 1.   This subject is far too broad. it might be narrowed by defining the university's role in a specific field, such as researching solar energy for use in homes.

   2.   This subject could be adequately treated in a short essay.

   3.   Because of the number of Shakespearean characters, this subject is too large. It might be narrowed to one or two characters of one play.

4. Obviously, this subject covers too much ground.

5. A short paper might give a satisfactory overview of this hobby, but for a better essay the student might focus on some specific aspect, such as "how to find rare/older cards" or "how to assess the value of a baseball card" or "types of baseball cards."

6. This subject could be discussed in a short essay, though again the student might profit from focusing on some specific aspect or particular kind of gun-control laws—or the state/city they govern.

7. The most serious disadvantages would be covered in a short paper.

8. The various models and functions of computers are a complex subject, too broad for a brief essay.

9. This subject could be described adequately.

10. Once the subject is narrowed to a specific type of bike (e.g., mountain, road, touring), selecting a bicycle would be a good topic for a process paper.

B. You will, of course, receive a variety of suitable answers here. Be sure that the students narrow the subjects sufficiently instead of stopping halfway. For example, a student might be tempted to narrow "music" to "rock music" or "education" to "college," but these subjects are still too broad for a short essay. Better answers will be more specific: "music" to "R.E.M.'s latest album," "education" to "required courses," etc. If done properly, this exercise should show students that selecting and narrowing a subject is the first step to discovering the main purpose of their essays. Once this step is mastered, students should find that formulating a thesis is not the difficult problem they might have imagined.

Practice, p. 25

The radio audience will want details about the supposed benefits of Breatharianism, even though the students may be skeptical and probably think Brooks is a phony. All the better then to place themselves in the persona of a gullible consumer, but at the same time to keep the assignment realistic by including some references like "Sure, I know you are probably skeptical," which shows an awareness of an audience that is not composed of complete boobs and which makes the ad more believable.

The parade permit application would try to show that these people are not completely crazy and would not pose a threat to public order. Moreover, this might lead to more business for the community as well as a sense that the town was interested in the health and welfare of its citizens and even the environment.

In the report, students can let go with their criticism and finally write for the side they were probably on all along. Details like a nutritional study showing the bad effects this diet would have on health, a record of Brooks's activity in other states and cities, and some personal testimony from other former Breatharians all would strengthen a case that seems sewed up already, so students win need to remember to do more than just say, "He's obviously guilty; let's leave it at that!"

Chapter 2: The Thesis Statement
p. 33

SUMMARY

What Is a Thesis? What Does a "Working Thesis" Do?

Can a "Working Thesis" Change?

Guidelines for Writing a Good Thesis
—state the writer's clearly defined opinion on some subject
—assert one main idea
—have something worthwhile to say
—limit thesis to fit the assignment
—state thesis clearly in specific terms
—locate thesis clearly, often in first or second paragraph

Avoiding Common Errors in thesis Statements
Don't:
—make it merely an announcement or a description
—clutter it with expressions like "In my opinion
—be unreasonable
—merely state a fact
—express your thesis in the form of a question

Practice, p. 42

Using the Essay Map
Practice, p. 46

ANSWERS TO "PRACTICE" EXERCISES

Practice, p. 42

A. 1.   Inadequate. It is unnecessary to say "I think," and "interesting" is too broad to have much meaning. What is it about the movie that is interesting—the subject, the acting, the cinematography? A good thesis is more specific.

2. Inadequate. First, a thesis should be expressed in a declarative sentence, not in a question. Second, comparing Japanese automobiles to American automobiles is too broad.

3. Inadequate. This is merely a statement that "some people" have this opinion. The purpose of a paper on this subject, however, is to reveal and support the author's opinion.

4. Inadequate. "My essay will tell you" is unnecessary.

5. Adequate. This specific assertion will lead to a discussion of the reasons why final examinations should be given before the Winter break.

6. Inadequate. It is not necessary to mention that the tuition increase will be a "terrible" burden. This thesis also has two parts that need to be separated: what, exactly, the extra burden of a tuition increase is, and what that has to do with the quality of education.

7. Inadequate. The writer's point is unclear. Does she believe body piercing should be illegal, or is it merely unsightly? It is also unclear whether the writer is unable to look people in the face who are "into body piercing" or if she finds facial piercing particularly offensive.

8. Inadequate. This statement carries an opinion too far. More specific and less extreme criticisms would make for a more reasonable paper.

9. Adequate.

10. Inadequate. The phrase "very important" is too vague. The thesis should assert a specific idea, such as "Having a close friend you can talk to makes adjusting to dorm living a lot easier."

B. These weak or faulty theses may be rewritten in a variety of ways; the comments below are intended to help you identify the problem with each example.

1. "Negative experience" is too broad; students should substitute specific description.

2. This thesis tries to argue two issues that would require two or three different kinds of supporting evidence. The rewritten thesis should be limited to one idea.

3. This is a "so what" thesis. Students should either take a stand on the issue

or state why it is important for the reader to know the advantages and disadvantages.

4. "One big headache" is too vague.

5. Students should omit the phrase "In this paper I will debate." Also, the writer's position should be clear.

6. Too vague. What is it we need to do about billboard clutter?

7. What is missing from this thesis statement is a purpose. Why do the insurance laws need to be rewritten? Which laws?

8. Too vague. What kind of bicycle riding? In what way is it good for the rider?

9. "In my opinion" can be deleted, and "fantastic" is too vague.

10. Too broad. What effects did the Civil Rights Movement have? Were they positive or negative? Both?

Practice, p. 46

A. 1. because of its . . . innovative editing.

2. Such a move . . . highway maintenance.

3. To guarantee . . . personalized design.

4. because it's . . . more luxurious.

5. To qualify . . . and training.

6. Through . . . squads.

7. Because . . . fatty tissue.

8. deductions . . . will be taxed.

9. They're . . . fun to grow.

10. His spirit of protest . . . arrangements.

B. Student responses will vary.

CHAPTER 3: THE BODY PARAGRAPHS
P. 51

SUMMARY

PLANNING THE BODY OF YOUR ESSAY
   —informal outlines

COMPOSING THE BODY PARAGRAPHS

THE TOPIC SENTENCE
   —supports the thesis by clearly stating a main point in the discussion
   —announces what the paragraph will be about
   —controls the subject matter of the paragraph
Focusing your topic sentence
Placing your topic sentence

Practice, p. 61

PARAGRAPH DEVELOPMENT
   —include enough information to make readers understand the topic sentence
   —make the information clear and specific

PARAGRAPH LENGTH
   —long enough to accomplish its purpose; short enough to be interesting
   —avoid the one- or two-sentence paragraph
   —divide longish paragraphs at a logical point

Practice, p. 70

PARAGRAPH UNITY
   —stick to the subject

Practice, p. 74

PARAGRAPH COHERENCE
   —a recognizable ordering of information (time, space, deductive, inductive)
   —transition words and phrases
   —repetition of key words
   —pronouns substituted for key nouns
   —parallelism
   —using a variety of transition devices

Practice, p. 82

Paragraph Sequence

Transitions Between Paragraphs

ANSWERS TO "PRACTICE" EXERCISES

Practice, p. 61

A. 1. Denim is one of America's

2. Adlai Stevenson, American statesman . . .

   "Stevenson was also admired . . ." should be crossed out.

3. Cooking in a microwave . . .

   Microwaves may be expensive . . . (concluding sentence)

4. almost every wedding tradition . . . weddings may vary . . . (concluding sentence)

5. In actuality, the most popular instrument . . .

6. The wonderful institution. . . .

B. 1. In the past year I have become much more outgoing at parties.

2. Jim's blind date turned out to be more of an expert at baseball cards than he was.

3. The movie's presentation of computer-generated special effects was a brilliant technical achievement.

4. The Memorial Day celebration had many more contests and prizes than last year.

5. I was tense around her parents, which made me clumsy all evening.

C. Your students should add topic sentences that resemble the following:

1. Many brilliant thinkers were not good students.

2. Most of the inexpensive trinkets sold when Elvis Presley was a popular rock star have now become much more valuable.

3. While an author's book or play may be respected by the public, the writer in person often receives little appreciation.

4. Although we tend to think of "record seasons" in terms of victorious teams, losing seasons are also permanently recorded in the annals of football.

D. Student responses will vary.

Practice, p. 70

1. The extremely vague adjectives (best, interesting, concerned, great) are the first clue that is paragraph is unfocused. The paragraph might target one of Wilson's strengths, then explain and illustrate it. Also, the reader-oriented purpose of this paragraph is puzzling.

2. Here there are generalized complaints about advice columns that are repetitious and go off in several directions. The solution is to focus on one idea, such as that the advice is out of touch with today's world, and then use examples to support this assertion.

3. This is another general survey of the topic that needs more concrete development to make it more coherent and tie it more closely to the topic sentence.

4. The topic sentence here—"Nursing homes are often sad places"—says it all. The rest of the paragraph is merely a repetition of that fact in different words.

5. While the writer has a clear distinction in mind between acquaintances and friends, trite and overused generalities ("being close to you" "sharing intimate things" "happy about being alive") add no real development to the paragraph. Also, using "you" in the hypothetical examples is ineffective; detailed, real personal or observed examples would be much more compelling.

Practice, p. 74

Delete the following sentences from the sample paragraphs:

1. During this period, songwriters . . .

2. Another well-known incident of cannibalism in the West occurred . . .

3. To publicize his new product . . . (Some readers might also consider the last sentence a break, though it might be seen as additional information to conclude the paragraph.)

4. U.S. Representative from Colorado . . . (to end of paragraph)

5. This example illustrates a drift from the original topic (dorm living providing a good way to meet people) into a new, slightly different topic (new friends teach students to get along with people from foreign countries). The writer might use the friend from Peru as an example of her original position, but overall she needs to rewrite the last half of her paragraph to bring it in line with her topic sentence.

Practice, p. 82

A. The first paragraph, on the apartment, is ordered by space, with the point of view moving from the left of the front door to the back of the room to the right of the door.

The second paragraph, on acts of greeting, is ordered chronologically, with details selected from the seventeenth-century tip through today.

The third paragraph, on exams, is ordered by parallelism, with sentences structured in the repeated pattern of "synonym for students + verb."

B. The transitional devices in each paragraph are underlined:

1. Each year I follow a system when preparing firewood to use in my stove. First, I hike about a mile from my house with my bow saw in hand. I then select three good size oak trees and mark them with orange ties. Next, I saw through the base of each tree about two feet from the ground. After I fell the trees, not only do I trim away the branches, but I also sort the scrap from the usable limbs. I find cutting the trees into manageable length logs is too much for one day; however, I roll them off the ground so they will not begin to rot. The next day I cut the trees into eight-foot lengths, which allows me to handle them more easily. Once they are cut, I roll them along the fire lane to the edge of the road where I stack them neatly but not too high. The next day I borrow my uncle's van, drive to the pile of logs, and load as many logs as I can, thus reducing the number of trips. When I finally have all the logs in my backyard, I begin sawing them into eighteen-inch lengths. I create large piles that consequently have to be split and finally stacked. The logs will age and dry until winter when I will make daily trips to the woodpile.

2. Fans of professional baseball and football argue continually over which is America's favorite spectator sport. Though the figures on attendance for each

vary with every new season, certain arguments remain the same, spelling out both the enduring appeals of each game and something about the people who love to watch. <u>Football, for instance,</u> is a quicker, more physical <u>sport,</u> and football <u>fans</u> enjoy the emotional involvement <u>they</u> feel while watching. <u>Baseball, on the other hand,</u> seems more mental, like chess, and attracts those <u>fans</u> who prefer a quieter, more complicated <u>game.</u> <u>In addition,</u> professional football teams usually play no more than fourteen <u>games</u> a year, providing fans with a whole week between games to work themselves up to a pitch of excitement and expectation. <u>Baseball</u> teams, <u>however,</u> play almost every day for six months, so that the typical baseball <u>fan</u> is not so crushed by missing a <u>game,</u> knowing there will be many other chances to attend. <u>Finally,</u> football <u>fans</u> seem to love the halftime pageantry, the marching bands, and the pretty cheerleaders, <u>whereas</u> baseball <u>fans</u> are more content to concentrate on the <u>game's</u> finer details and spend the breaks between innings filling out their own private scorecards.

C. The choice of transition words may vary slightly from student to student, but here is a typical response to the dinosaur paragraph:

dinosaurs, then, Because, reptiles, however, although, dinosaurs, they, as well as, Another, dinosaurs, In addition, dinosaurs, also, dinosaurs, therefore, monsters, other, scientists, dinosaurs, or, or.

D. The sentences in Paragraph One should be grouped in this order: 7, 8, 2, 6, 4, 1, 3, 5

The sentences in Paragraph Two should be grouped in this order: 6, 3, 7, 9, 8, 4, 2, 1, 5

CHAPTER 4: BEGINNINGS AND ENDINGS
P. 89

SUMMARY

HOW TO WRITE A GOOD LEAD-IN
—a paradoxical or intriguing statement
—an arresting statistic or shocking statement
—a question
—a quotation or literary allusion
—a relevant story, joke, or anecdote
—a description, often used for emotional appeal
—a factual statement or summary who-what-where-when-why lead-in
—an analogy or comparison
—a contrast
—a personal experience
—a catalog of relevant examples
—a statement of a problem or a popular misconception

AVOIDING ERRORS IN LEAD-INS
—make sure your lead-in introduces your thesis
—make it brief
—don't begin with an apology or complaint
—don't assume your audience already knows your subject matter
—stay clear of overused lead-ins

Practice, p. 94

HOW TO WRITE A GOOD CONCLUDING PARAGRAPH
—a restatement of both the thesis and the essay's major points
—an evaluation of the importance of the essay's subject
—a statement of the essay's broader implications
—a call to action
—a prophecy or warning based on the essay's thesis
—a witticism that emphasizes or sums up the point of the essay
—a quotation, story, or joke that emphasizes or sums up the point of the essay
—an image or description that lends finality to the essay
—a rhetorical question that makes the reader think about the essay's main point
—a forecast based on the essay's thesis

37

Avoiding Errors in Conclusions
—avoid a mechanical ending
—don't introduce new points
—don't tack on a conclusion
—don't change your stance
—avoid trite expressions

Practice, p. 97

How to Write a Good Title

ANSWERS TO "PRACTICE" EXERCISES

Practice, p. 94.

Student responses will vary.

Practice, p. 97.

Student responses will vary.

Chapter 5: Drafting and Revising: Creative Thinking, Critical Thinking
p. 101

SUMMARY

WHAT IS REVISION?

WHEN DOES REVISION OCCUR?

MYTHS ABOUT REVISION
—revision is not autopsy
—revision is not limited to editing or proofreading
—revision is not punishment or busy work

CAN I LEARN TO IMPROVE MY REVISION SKILLS?

PREPARING TO DRAFT AND REVISE

YOU CAN ALWAYS CHANGE YOUR DRAFT:
—write on only one side of the paper
—leave big margins on both sides of each page
—devise a system of symbols to mark changes you wish to make
—leave blank spots to note areas needing further development
—use a line or x for corrections; don't scratch it out
—try to work from a typed copy
—always keep your drafts
Suggestions for writers with word processors

A REVISION PROCESS FOR YOUR DRAFTS
I. Revise for purpose, thesis, and audience

II. Revise your ideas and evidence

—What is critical thinking?
—Thinking critically as a writer
distinguish fact from opinion
support opinions with evidence
evaluate strength of evidence
use enough specific supporting evidence

39

watch for biases/emotions that undermine evidence
check evidence for logical fallacies

III.   Revise for organization

IV.   Revise for clarity and style

V.   Edit for errors

—read aloud
—know your own punctuation/grammar weaknesses
—read backwards
—learn "tricks" for treating some punctuation/grammar problems
—eliminate common mistakes
—use reference tools

VI.   Proofreading

A FINAL CHECKLIST FOR YOUR ESSAY

BENEFITING FROM REVISION WORKSHOPS
As writer:
—develop a constructive attitude
—come prepared
—evaluate suggestions carefully
—find the good in bad advice
As reviewer:
—develop a constructive attitude
—be clear and specific
—address important issues
—encourage the writer
—understand the role of the critical reader

Practice, p. 120

SOME LAST ADVICE: HOW TO PLAY WITH YOUR MENTAL BLOCKS
—give yourself as much time as possible
—try verbalizing your ideas
—break the paper into manageable bits
—get the juices flowing and the pen moving
—set limits on the amount of time you'll write at one sitting
—give yourself permission to write garbage
—warm up by writing something else
—imagine writing to a friend

—remember that blocks are temporary, not permanent
—if you have a bright idea for another section, skip to it
—do something else for a while
—remember that nobody does it perfectly the first time

ANSWERS TO "PRACTICE" EXERCISES

Practice, p. 120

These two essays lend themselves to a variety of assignments. The students might mark them at home and then discuss them in class, rewrite them on the board or in groups, or rewrite them individually at home. The comments below are intended for use as guidelines, not as a complete set of corrections.

A. "DORM LIFE"

The writer has not mastered the basic concepts of organization, development, unity, or coherence.

Paragraph 1: the writer's attitude is clear, although a better essay might present a more interesting lead-in. The diction of the last sentence ("illusions, erroneous perceptions of reality") is overblown.

Paragraph 2: the paragraph begins abruptly and needs focusing. The sentences describing the girls' reactions are headed in the right direction but need developing; the sentence containing speculation on the girls' motives seems out of place. The last sentence's reference to "the guys seem nice" contradicts the thesis idea of unfriendly people.

Paragraph 3: No transition from paragraph 2 makes this one begin abruptly, also. The discussion here is extremely repetitive and wordy and does contain obvious breaks in unity (music she likes, where they study, wishes for consideration). Clichés also abound (wee hours of morning, ears ringing, stomach churning). The writer needs to be encouraged to condense her complaint and to focus on providing additional specific examples, such as the one about the neighbors playing Metallica and Nirvana.

Paragraph 4: Again, no smooth transition to her next point. Since the writer wanted "wild parties," it's up to her to explain in more detail why the two mentioned here failed to qualify. A large crowd and the smell of roast pig do not necessarily mean the parties were failures. Perhaps the lack of parties is more to the point. At any rate, the conclusion of the paragraph again drifts away from the original subject.

Paragraph 5: No transition to the main point, which directly contradicts her thesis. She breaks unity with the two sentences on orange juice, but the examples of the food may contain her best details in the essay (even though they're wordy and expressed in clichés such as "mystery meat").

Paragraph 6: the conclusion is happy-face fluff that ignores the real complaints voiced throughout her essay.

B. "MAYBE YOU SHOULDN'T GO AWAY TO COLLEGE"

This student also needs help with organization, paragraph development and unity, and sentence construction. The comparison of the local school to the out-of-town school should be made much clearer in each body paragraph through the addition of specific examples.

Paragraph 1: the thesis is clear but the essay map is expressed awkwardly.

Paragraph 2: the contrast between the cost of attending an out-of-town college and living at home needs a clearer statement in the topic sentence. How can the writer know that out-of-town colleges always have higher tuition? Perhaps it would be more effective to discuss the expense of transportation rather than tuition, which varies from school to school regardless of location. The example of room and board should be developed further.

Paragraph 3: This sentence seems off the subject; omit the paragraph.

Paragraph 4: This paragraph does have a point, but the writer needs to focus and clarify what kinds of "changes" she means. Development of the paragraph should be improved by adding some specific examples of the pressures and changes involved in going away to college; the writer could then show how the security of home could make such changes easier.

Paragraphs 5 and 6: these two paragraphs discuss the same point and therefore need to be combined. However, instead of merely asking whether students should be forced to break away at this time, the writer should persuasively argue her own position, perhaps by explaining some of the responsibilities of living away at college. (She also needs to make sure that her discussion of "responsibilities" does not merely repeat the discussion of "pressures" in paragraph 4. Are these two points really different? If they aren't, her essay map also needs rethinking.)

Paragraph 7: the conclusion is unnecessarily brief, although the writer does try to end on a play on words ("right road" and "just around the corner").

Chapter 6: Effective Sentences
p. 127

SUMMARY

Develop a Clear Style
  —give your sentences content
  —make your sentences specific
  —keep them simple
  —pay attention to word order
  —avoid mixed constructions and faulty predication

Develop a Concise Style
  —avoid deadwood constructions
  —avoid redundancy
  —carefully consider your passive verbs
  —avoid pretentiousness

Practice, p. 140

Develop a Lively Style
  —use specific, descriptive verbs
  —use specific, precise modifiers that help the reader see, hear, or feel what you
    are describing
  —emphasize people when possible
  —vary your sentence style
  —avoid overuse of any one kind of construction in the same sentence
  —don't change your point of view between or within sentences

Practice, p. 146

Develop an Emphatic Style
  —word order
  —coordination
  —subordination

Practice, p. 152

ANSWERS TO "PRACTICE" EXERCISES

Practice, p. 140

A. 1. Roger's marketing skills made him important to his company's sales department.

2. The new detective show on TV stars Phil Noir and is set in the 1940s.

3. The floor of Sarah's room was always cluttered with dolls, clothes, game pieces, books, and old candy wrappers.

4. *Biofeedback: How to Stop It* has so many funny and sarcastic comments about California self-help fads, I couldn't put it down.

5. Proponents of capital punishment believe it deters criminals and reduces the cost of incarceration.

6. I get several pieces of junk mail each day hawking everything from apple corers to zipper repair kits.

7. At my local college, I've signed up for a class in "Cultivating Mold in Your Refrigerator for Fun and Profit."

8. Your horoscope may not be accurate, but reading it can be entertaining.

9. Lois Mueller, the author of *The Underachiever's Guide to Very Small Business Opportunities* and *Whine Your Way to Success,* is having an autograph party at the campus bookstore today at noon.

10. From the expression on everyone's faces, the speaker was clearly not welcome.

B. 1. If you are accosted in the subway at night, go to the police to learn ways of avoiding such incidents.

2. You are desperate if you try to lose weight through Pyramid Power.

3. I miss my dog that has been dead almost five years now.

4. For sale: Unique, hard-to-find handmade gifts for that special person in your life.

5. After putting off surgery for years, I finally had my leg operated on during Thanksgiving break.

6. We need to hire two nonsmoking teachers for the three-year-old preschool kids.

7. The story of Rip Van Winkle illustrates the dangers of oversleeping.

8. We gave our unwanted waterbed to our friends.

9. Neither people who are allergic to chocolate nor children under 6 should be given the new vaccine.

10. At 7 AM in her luxurious bathroom, Brenda starts preparing for another busy day as an executive.

C. 1. He lost the editing job because of his careless and sloppy proofreading.

2. Some of the Prehistoric History professors are incompetent.

3. My older brother can't drive to work this week because he wrecked his car early Saturday morning.

4. Today we often criticize advertising that demeans women by presenting them unfairly.

5. The attorney defending the twin brothers objected to the prosecutor's attempt to introduce the antique gun.

6. In "Now Is the Winter of Our Discount Tent," the poet expresses her disgust with camping.

7. Although the boss appeared to be listening, we didn't think he took our concerns seriously.

8. Learning word processing makes you a more efficient worker.

9. Some people assert their superiority by being rude to servers at restaurants.

10. To improve my chances for promotion, I decided to try to marry the boss's daughter.

Practice, p. 146

A. 1. After listening to the whining moan of the reactor, I'm not sure that nuclear power as we know it has a future.

2. The City Council was embarrassed because the application forms for grants to fund tourist development activities were mailed without stamps.

3. Watching Jim Bob eat pork chops was nauseating.

4. For sale: elegant antique bureau with thick legs and extra-large side handles. Suitable for use by ladies or gentlemen.

5. The workshop on family relationships we are attending is helpful because we learn to control our parents through blackmail and guilt.

6. faint, and left me with a headache and rubber knees.

7. demanded, immediately

8. The wild oats soup was so delicious we slurped it all down in five minutes.

9. leaped toward the judging stand for his ribbon

10. My roommate is eccentric but he's very loyal to his friends.

B. Student responses will vary.

Practice, p. 152

A. 1. Joe Louis, one-time heavyweight boxing champion, once said, "I don't really like money but it quiets my nerves."

2. According to recent polls, most Americans get their news from television.

3. Of all the world's problems, the most urgent is hunger.

4. Of all the foreign countries I visited last year, my favorite was Greeces.

5. One habit I will not tolerate is knuckle-cracking.

B. 1. The guru rejected his dentist's offer of novocaine because he could transcend dental medication.

2. Because John incorrectly identified Harper Lee as the author of the south-of-the-border classic *Tequila Mockingbird,* he failed his literature test.

3. Dr. Acula, who specializes in acupuncture in the neck, recently opened a new office.

4. Although the police had only a few clues, they suspected that Jean and David had strangled each other in a desperate struggle over control of the thermostat.

5. Described by one critic as a "pinhead chiller," *Sorority Babes in the Slimeball Bowl-o-rama* (1988) is Bubba's favorite movie.

6. Because their menu includes banana split personality, repressed duck, shrimp basket case, and self-expresso, we're going to the Psychoanalysis Restaurant.

7. Kato lost the junior high spelling bee when he couldn't spell *DNA.*

8. Colorado hosts an annual BobFest to honor all persons named Bob, and events include playing softbob, bobbing for apples, listening to bob-pipes, and eating bob-e-que.

9. When the earthquake shook the city, Louise was performing primal scream therapy. (Or: Because Louise was performing primal-scream therapy, an earthquake shook the city!)

10. In 1789 many Parisians bought a new perfume called "Guillotine" because they wanted to be on the cutting edge of fashion.

C. Obviously, the sentences may be combined in many ways. Here are some examples.

1. While living on a raft on the Mississippi River, a runaway boy, accompanied by an escaped slave, has many adventures and learns valuable lessons about friendship and human kindness.

2. A young man returning from prison joins his family in their move from the Dust Bowl to California, where they find intolerance and dishonest employers instead of jobs.

3. A mad scientist who wants to re-create life makes a gruesome monster in his laboratory but is killed by his rebellious creature as the villagers, in revolt, storm the castle.

CHAPTER 7: WORD LOGIC
P. 157

SUMMARY

SELECTING THE CORRECT WORDS
Accuracy
    —confused words
    —idiomatic phrases
Levels of Language
    —colloquial
    —informal
    —formal
Tone
    —invective
    —sarcasm
    —irony
    —flippancy or cuteness
    —sentimentality
    —preachiness
    —pomposity
Connotation and Denotation

Practice, p. 164

SELECTING THE BEST WORDS
    —make them as precise as possible
    —make them as fresh and original as possible
    —don't use trendy expressions or slang
    —select simple, direct words your readers can easily understand
    —call things by their proper names
    —avoid sexist language
    —enliven your writing with figurative language when appropriate
    —vary your word choice so that your prose does not sound wordy, repetitious, or monotonous
    —remember that wordiness is a major problem for all writers

Practice, p. 176

ANSWERS TO "PRACTICE" EXERCISES

Practice, p. 164

A. 1. foul

2. who's, photographic, accepted, number, compliments

3. It's, too, their, they're

4. two weeks, two friends, too short, too tired, you're, too broke

5. regardless, course

6. ants

7. lose, your, metal, its

8. council, affect

B. 1. The sunset signaled the cat to come out for its nightly prowl.

2. I disagree with the President's Mideast peace plan.

3. I wanted information about the poor.

4. If the bill to legalize marijuana is passed, we think most Americans will soon be smoking it.

5. I enjoy watching white mice.

C. The word with the most pleasing connotation is on the left, the least pleasing on the right. Opinions may vary.

1. quiet/drab or boring

2. slender/anorexic

3. famous/notorious or infamous

4. affluent/privileged

5. educator/lecturer

D. 1. aroma

2. voluptuous single woman

3. strict

4. concern

5. expert, presentation, older gentleman

6. unusual

7. competent

8. distinctive, unemployed

9. religious beliefs

10. led

Practice, p. 176

A. Everyone, of course, will have different responses, but here are some suggestions:

1. The chemical experiment killed all the fish in the river.

2. The guest speaker's references to religious cults were inappropriate for a prom banquet.

3. The 50-room mausoleum was rotting away and covered with tacky trim and ornaments.

4. Our father likes to spend time helping us and entertaining us with stories from his childhood.

5. Sandbagging our riverfront property was exhausting, but it brought the neighbors closer together.

6. My new lawnmower came without a handle.

7. Mother Theresa was more dedicated than most of us to helping the poor.

8. The biology textbook was boring.

9. I could hear the baby screaming a block away,

10. For only three dollars we got eighteen appetizers, five main courses, and fifteen desserts at the Yugoslavian restaurant.

B. 1. When my mother didn't return from the bathroom we were upset.

2. According to former-President Jimmy Carter, the hostage rescue mission in Iran was a failure.

3. On election day, everyone eighteen or older should vote.

4. No matter what measures are taken, cowboys and farmers will continue to have difficulty making money.

5. Officers in the Armed Forces realize that someday they may have to go to war in a third-world country.

6. Although he once thought she was sincere, he then realized she was deceitful.

7. Your apple pie is so delicious that any good cook would be jealous.

8. The City Councilman was furious to learn that his son had been arrested for embezzling funds from the low-income housing project.

9. After the policemen arrested the protesters, some of the reporters who had been watching the riot were murdered.

10. The automobile company sent a letter to all Gator X42s owners praising the car's vinyl interior, but warning that the X42s had been recalled as its defective steering system could cause the driver to lose control of the vehicle.

C. 1. For good health, use a toothpick daily and avoid tanning salons.

2. According to the military, you should not attempt a predawn jump without a parachute from an airplane since you would crash into the ground. (This is only a best guess; some jargon is so convoluted that any number of interpretations is possible.)

3. American Airlines' passengers can now take a shuttle to and from their flights.

4. If you are in the military, you should avoid being shot and killed.

5. The U.S. Embassy in Budapest warned its employees that friendly local women might actually be Hungarian agents.

6. "I thought the evening would be rewarding but my blind date was unattractive and had an unpleasant disposition, so I went home early," said Wayne, who was not an appealing person himself.

7. The employee was fired because she was rude and lazy.

8. My college announced today that all classes will be delayed and perhaps postponed indefinitely because of lack of funds.

9. All of us could understand Mabel's essay on the effect of the decreased tax base on funding for education.

10. According to Admiral Wesley L. MacDonald, U.S. intelligence was not monitoring action in Grenada until just prior to the United States' 1983 invasion.

CHAPTER 8: THE READING-WRITING CONNECTION
P. 181

SUMMARY

HOW CAN READING WELL HELP ME BECOME A BETTER WRITER?

HOW CAN I BECOME AN ANALYTICAL READER?

Steps to Reading Well

1—before reading the essay, note publication information and biographical data on the author
2—note the title of the essay
3—read the essay-noting any key ideas and referring to the dictionary as desired—then briefly summarize your impression of the essay
4—review the title and introductory paragraphs again
5—locate and mark the thesis
6—locate and mark supporting points or ideas
7—note how the writer develops, explains, or argues each supporting point
8—practice using marginal symbols to mark points of interest
9—review the essay's organization
10—review the unity and coherence of the essay, noting transitions
11—consider the writer's style and the essay's tone

Practice, p. 189

ANSWERS TO "PRACTICE" EXERCISES

Practice, p, 189.

Student responses will vary.

PART TWO
PURPOSES, MODES, AND STRATEGIES

CHAPTER 9: EXPOSITION
P. 193

SUMMARY

THE STRATEGIES OF EXPOSITION

STRATEGY ONE: DEVELOPMENT BY EXAMPLE
 —examples support, clarify, interest, and persuade
 —examples can be brief
 —they can be extended
 —examples hold the reader's attention
 —they can be used in all types of writing
Questions for Essay Development:
 —are all my examples relevant?
 —are they well chosen?
 —are there enough to make each point clear and persuasive?
Problems to Avoid:
 —a lack of specific detail
 —a lack of coherence

STRATEGY TWO: DEVELOPMENT BY PROCESS ANALYSIS
 —directional versus informative
 —steps for essay development
  select an appropriate subject
  describe any necessary equipment and define special terms
  state steps in a logical, chronological order
   explain each step clearly, sufficiently, accurately
   organize your steps effectively
Problems to Avoid:
 —don't forget to include a thesis
 —pay special attention to the conclusion

STRATEGY THREE: DEVELOPMENT BY COMPARISON AND CONTRAST
—"Point-by-point" method
—"block" method
Problems to Avoid:
—the "so what" thesis is the most serious error
—describe your subjects clearly and distinctly
—avoid a choppy essay

STRATEGY FOUR: DEVELOPMENT BY DEFINITION
—dictionary
—extended
We define in order to clarify a term that is:
—vague, controversial, or misunderstood
—abstract
—new or unusual (slang, dialect, or jargon)
—unfamiliar
—used to entertain by presenting its interesting history, uses, or effects
Developing Your Essay:
—know your purpose
—give your readers a reason to read
—keep your audience in mind to anticipate and avoid problems of clarity
—use as many strategies as necessary to clarify your definition
Problems to Avoid:
Don't:
—present an incomplete definition
—introduce your essay with a quotation from *Webster's*
—define vaguely or by using generalities
—offer circular definitions

STRATEGY FIVE: DEVELOPMENT BY DIVISION AND CLASSIFICATION
Division Versus Classification
Developing Your Essay:
—select one principle of classification or division and stick to it
—state the purpose of your division or classification
—account for all the parts in your division or classification

STRATEGY SIX: DEVELOPMENT BY CAUSAL ANALYSIS
Developing Your Essay:
—present a reasonable thesis statement
—limit your essay to a discussion of recent, major causes or effects
—organize your essay clearly
—convince your reader that a causal relationship exists by showing how the relationship works

Problems to Avoid:
  —don't oversimplify
  —avoid the post hoc fallacy
  —avoid circular logic

DISCUSSION, ANSWERS TO QUESTIONS, VOCABULARY

1. EXAMPLE

"SO WHAT'S SO BAD ABOUT BEING SO-SO?"—P. 204

Discussion

Strick's essay, originally published in 1984, appeared at a time of heightened aware-ness of the competitiveness of American society. Do college students of the 1990s still perceive overzealous competition as a problem in the U.S.? A lively discussion could result by asking students to agree or disagree with Strick's contention that "in today's competitive world we have to be 'experts.'" Ask them to support their views with spe-cific examples in the same manner that Strick supports her thesis. Consider having students compare this essay to Zinsser's "College Pressures." How do the essays com-plement each other? Do students agree with the combined views of these writers?

Answers to Questions

1. It is an example that introduces the thesis.

2. The thesis is implied throughout the essay, but is stated clearly and without equivocation in the next-to-last paragraph: "I think it's time we put a stop to all this . . . and . . . enjoy being a beginner again." Our many leisure-time activities were meant to be enjoyed, not necessarily mastered.

3. The major examples are from sports; perhaps more could have been offered from school. The first, running, refers to the pervasive concern for and availability of equipment. In this case, it is the right shoes, another area of specialization that wasn't a concern in the old days when anything to protect your feet would do. The dancing example continues the emphasis on the proper costume, the correct look, for specialized activities. The next three, knitting, soccer, and lessons, illus-trate the effect of competition on attitudes rather than externals.

4. Too much competition drains the fun out of an experience. Her piano playing irritates her son, running without the proper equipment is an embarrassment to serious athletes, "real" dancers don't just mess around with a few steps, and if children can't attain a high level of expertise in soccer, gymnastics, and foreign languages, it is as if their time and effort were wasted. Children don't seem to be

able to have fun anymore, as reflected by the daughter in paragraph 8 who muses, "Well, I don't actually have a lot of free time."

5. In paragraph 4, informal verbs like "pulling on" your sneakers and "slogging" are in contrast to formal ones like "plan" and "log." In addition, the mention of "leather or canvas," the type of sole, and the brand of shoe are nice contrasts to her image of an earlier time when a concern for such fine points was unnecessary. Paragraph 6 has a long sentence full of details about the reindeer sweater. The form of the sentence reinforces the point Strick is making about how general knowledge is not sufficient; these days you have to add all sorts of little touches that demonstrate your great skill. A sentence in paragraph 8 is similar, only this time the subject is early childhood education; in addition to soccer lessons at age three, Strick throws in parenthetical references to preschool diving, creative writing, and Suzuki clarinet. All three refer to early education, but the examples Strick chooses seem frivolous or unnecessary and reinforce the sarcastic tone of her essay. Most of the other paragraphs have a similar depth and breadth of detail.

6. Dialogue makes the points of the essay more real and personal. It's fine to criticize a lifestyle, but maybe the author is overly picky or is isolated from mainstream, middle-of-the road culture. Quotations from real people tend to soften this impression and give the essay the feel of a documentary.

7. The solution is to take up an activity without ever intending to become good at it. This change in attitude seems naive and yet at the same time a relief from the competitive atmosphere Strick has described. Strick uses the example of two-year-olds to give adults an idea of how to change their attitude and get on the road to a so-so lifestyle. Presumably, two-year-olds have not yet been infected with that competitive spirit.

8. Although there are many occasions when Strick is humorous, overall the tone of the essay is that of a person who is genuinely concerned about the way we live our lives and wants us to change our habits. She uses phrases like "Have you noticed?" or "We used to do these things for fun," and she even acknowledges that what she is criticizing has some merit ("Ambition, drive and the desire to excel are all admirable within limits."), all of which gives her suggestions and point of view credibility. Since this is not a scholarly treatise intended for presentation at a conference of sociology professors, the breezy informality of the piece will be more interesting to a general reader. Also, since many of these readers are deeply affected by the lifestyle Strick describes, her gently humorous but pointed comments are more likely to be taken seriously; Strick seems to be the neighbor we all have or are, and we share her concerns as well as her frustration.

9. The conclusion wraps up the essay by putting into practice (not too much, of course!) the process Strick has just suggested: take up an activity with no intention of becoming good at it.

10. Student agreement/disagreement should be well supported with specific textual examples.

Vocabulary

1. errant (2)—roving, straying, wandering

2. incompetence (3)—lack of necessary ability

3. aficionados (4)—enthusiastic admirers or followers

4. mediocrity (4)—average to below-average ability

5. excel (9)—to surpass or do better than others

6. fluent (9)—flowing smoothly or gracefully; most often used to describe those who speak and write foreign languages well

7. zest (11)—spirited enjoyment; gusto

2. PROCESS ANALYSIS

"TO BID THE WORLD FAREWELL"—P. 219

Discussion

Mitford's essay shows students that process papers can have a purpose beyond the simple spreading of "how-to-do-it" information. Students will frequently become involved in a debate over Mitford's belief that this "prettying up" of the dead is excessive and absurd, with some arguing that the elaborate funeral ritual is essential for the living and others attacking it as sham. Such a debate might lead some students to investigate the legal burial requirements in their state and then to write an essay about their findings. And while many students find this essay distasteful, most agree that Mitford has performed a valuable service by publicizing the process so that people have enough information to make a choice regarding their own funeral or that of relatives. This essay provides an excellent opportunity to discuss use of vivid, sensory details and their effects on the reader. Mitford's carefully selected word choice ("the embalmer . . . returns to the attack") should be analyzed as the class discusses the essay's tone. This essay may also be used to introduce such terms as euphemism and personification; Mitford's easily recognized transition devices might emphasize a lesson on coherence.

Answers to Questions

1. Mitford feels that, in contrast to earlier days, Americans are now paying millions for a process they know nothing about. The reason is not the gruesomeness of the subject nor Americans' lack of curiosity, but the almost universal desire of undertakers to keep the process a secret. Mitford implies that if people did understand the embalming process, they might begin to question whether they wanted or needed such a service. Her attitude toward the morticians is critical; she obviously believes that people should have access to information on the embalming process.

2. Informative.

3. Yes. There are numerous examples of descriptions that appeal to the senses. Below are listed only a few:

   Sight: "Positioning the lips is a problem. The lips should give the impression of being ever so slightly parted. . . . Up drift can sometimes be remedied by pushing one or two straight pins through the inner margin of the lower lip and then inserting them between the two front upper teeth" (paragraph 9).

   Smell: "About three to six gallons of a dyed and perfumed solution of formaldehyde, glycerin, borax, phenol, alcohol and water is soon circulating through Mr. Jones . . ." (paragraph 9).

   Touch: "If Flextone is used . . . The skin retains a velvety softness, the tissues are rubbery and pliable" (paragraph 8).

4. Mitford wants her readers to identify and sympathize with the corpse, to understand that the body suffering such indignities was once a living person.

5. Mitford feels that this process is unnecessary, expensive, and degrading. Her tone may be described as ironic or sarcastic. To "have at" him makes Mr. Jones seem like a piece of meat, as does "returning to the attack" in the next example. "Friends will say. . ." exposes the fake piety of those who aren't really close to the deceased and can only comment on the embalmer's skill. The caution about the placement of the body mocks the undertaker's inappropriate elevation of a trivial concern in the context of grieving survivors, and the sarcastic "Here he will hold open house . . ." makes it sound like he is still alive.

6. She quotes the undertakers and textbooks to show the funeral business's crass and depersonalized treatment of the dead. They seem preoccupied with the need to artificially "beautify" the body, regardless of the means (kitchen cleanser and nail polish on the teeth, pins in the lips, wire through the jaw, etc.). The dead person becomes little more than a department store dummy to be dressed for some sort

of freak fashion show. Mitford quotes the undertakers themselves to show the readers that the callous descriptions are not her words but theirs. The quote in paragraph 7 says that even though research on embalming is "haphazard," undertakers are advised (for "best results") to begin embalming before life is "completely extinct," that is, before all the body's cells are dead. Mitford implies that undertakers might be so eager to achieve those best results that they might begin too soon; but she ironically concludes that at least there is no risk of accidentally burying anyone alive: after all, embalming removes the blood.

7. Mitford quotes such euphemisms to show how the funeral business tries to sugarcoat death for the living by pretending the dead person is only asleep or resting. Terms such as "dermasurgeon" and "restorative artist" are used to give embalmers more prestige by linking their work to that of physicians, especially plastic surgeons. The words in paragraph 10 connote a defenseless person being attacked by the mortician. The series of questions in paragraph 12 reproduces the flippant tone Mitford thinks characterizes the embalmer's attitude toward the bodies. The corpse is not a dead person worthy of respect but merely a challenge to the embalmer's ingenuity. One can almost hear Mitford's sarcastic imitation of a mortician saying, "Head off? Hey, no problem."

8. Yes. Beginning with paragraph 4: "first" (paragraphs 3–4); "preparation room" (4–5); "first," "embalming" (5–6); "another" (6–7); "to return to" (7–8); "soon," "Mr. Jones" (8–9); "The next step" (9–10); "all this attention" (10–11); "returns" (11–12); "The opposite condition" (12–13); parallel construction of "If Mr. Jones . . ." (14–15); "completed," "now" (15–16); "now ready" (16–17); "next" (17–18).

9. Yes. The idea of a corpse holding "open house" for visitors is ridiculous. But ridiculous, according to Mitford, is the correct term for what embalmers try to do: dress up and beautify a dead body as if it were hosting a party,

10. Some students may argue that the funeral business makes it easier for the living to accept the death of a friend or relative and that this comfort justifies the artificial "dandifying" of the body. Others may agree with Mitford, adding that the cost of funerals today is also unreasonable.

Vocabulary

1. docility (1)—meekness, obedience

2. perpetuation (1)—continuance

3. inherent (2)—basic, intrinsic

4. mandatory (2)—obligatory

5. intractable (3)—obstinate, not easily governed or controlled

6. reticence (3)—reluctance

7. raison d'être (3)—French for "reason to be"

8. ingenious (5)—brilliant

9. cadaver (5)—a dead body

10. somatic (7)—pertaining to, or affecting, the body

11. rudimentary (7)—basic, elementary

12. dispel (7)—remove

13. pliable (8)—easily bent, supple

14. semblance (11) form or outward appearance

15. ravages (11)—violently destructive effects

16. stippling (12)—painting by means of dots or small spots

17. emaciation (13)—wasted or depleted condition

3. COMPARISON/CONTRAST

"TWO WAYS OF VIEWING THE RIVER"—P. 236

Discussion

While many students will have read the novels of Samuel Clemens (Mark Twain), few of them may be familiar with his essays. "Two Ways of Viewing the River" is an intriguing piece for class discussion since rather than contrasting two different subjects, as is most often done (see "Grant and Lee: A Study in Contrasts"), Clemens presents two vastly different perspectives of the same subject. It might be emphasized that the actual features of the river remain the same (the sunset, the floating log); it is Clemens's vision of the river that has changed. Students might be asked to complete a timed in-class freewriting exercise in which they contrast two very different perspectives they have had of one, unchanging subject. For example, they might contrast their first impression with a later view of someone they now know well. Discussion of these student writings could reveal the importance of descriptive detail in comparison/contrast essays.

Answers to Questions

1. Clemens is contrasting his personal, emotional view of the river when he was new to steamboating with his later view as a captain. His thesis is embodied in the first three sentences: While a captain's perspective is valuable and gives a sense of accomplishment, it has sadly replaced forever an earlier, mystical connection to the river.

2. Clemens chooses the block method of development. One reason this choice is appropriate is that he can contrast the same observations (e.g., the floating log, the tall dead tree) in each block; a reader would not get lost in the points of contrast from block to block. A more significant reason that this is not only an appropriate choice, but also may be the best choice for this selection is that the first block sets a mood in its totality that is necessary to understand before the reader can understand the loss implied in the more sterile and cold second block.

3. The second sentence in paragraph 2 provides a transition for the reader. Clemens moves the reader ahead in time to a later view of the river "when I began to cease from noting the glories and the charms which the moon and the sun and the twilight wrought upon the river's face."

4. Clemens's reference to doctors in the final paragraph broadens the meaning of this excerpt. Not only was this an experience in his life, but he also suggests that the understanding might extend to a more universal experience.

5. The questions encourage the reader to think about a more universal application of Clemens's experience. The last question asks the reader to think further: is the loss of innocent wonder and splendor worth the gain of accomplishment and professionalism?

6. The language in paragraph 1 is rich, lush, sensual, and poetic. The diction appropriately creates the mood of wonder and magnificence for the reader to contrast to the more businesslike language of the second view.

7. ". . . as many-tinted as an opal . . ."

   ". . . trail that shone like silver."

   These similes provide a more visual image for the reader, e.g., the swirling, changing colors in an opal.

8. The language in paragraph 2 is more sparse and pictureless. The visions and feelings relative to the river are unimportant; only the usefulness of the objects and the dangers created by them are important to a good captain.

9. Clemens personifies the "new snag" when he claims it will "fish for steamboats." This personification adds a certain element of alienation and antagonism to his later view of the river which contrasts sharply to his earlier perspective.

10. While the mood of each contrasting block is distinctly different—the earlier block is warm and sensual while the latter is harsh and professional—the tone of the entire essay is rather consistent. Throughout the selection, Clemens has a sense of nostalgia and reflection over times and feelings gone forever.

Vocabulary

1. trifling (1)—being of small value or importance

2. acquisition (1)—something gained

3. conspicuous (1)—easy to see; attracting attention

4. ruddy (1)—reddish; glowing

5. wrought (2)—fashioned or made, usually with great care

6. compassing (3)—providing direction for

"GRANT AND LEE: A STUDY IN CONTRASTS"—*P. 238*

Discussion

This is one of the most famous (and most frequently anthologized) essays that students will come across. The author is well known for his encyclopedic knowledge of and writings about the Civil War, and this excerpt reflects not only that knowledge but also Catton's empathy for the period and many of the principal characters of that tragic conflict. It is also a concrete example of the three ways to avoid what Wyrick calls the "so what" thesis. The subject has a universal appeal—it demonstrates something about principled soldiers in a native American conflict that can apply to us all, even if we are not in a "war" but merely in an argument. It is directed to Americans interested in a vital part of our history, and it especially shows "a particular relationship between two subjects." The major method of organization—contrast—announces itself in the title, and the development is essentially by the "point-by-point" method. There is, however, some comparison at the end which provides not only some perspective, but an effective conclusion as well.

Answers to Questions

1. The thesis is contained in all of paragraph 3.

2. A good summary of Lee's view of society is in paragraph 5, where Catton states that Lee represented "the age of chivalry transplanted to a New World." The old idea of the Great Chain of Being is a good analogy to Lee's social ideal. Some were higher on the chain than others, but the higher-ups needed to see their favored position not as a justification for abusing the lower-downs, but as a position of responsibility from which they had the means and the power to improve society as a whole and not just their own lot in life. Catton describes Lee in terms that might also be applied to, say, the men of the Kennedy dynasty: the quintessential man of leisure whose concern for his version of society makes him not only a great defender of a humanitarian aristocracy, but an even greater symbol of what the South stood for and what Confederate soldiers were fighting for.

3. Catton describes Grant as both the product and the embodiment of the pioneers and the pioneer spirit. These people looked at the social structure of the country as virtually nonexistent, except as it promoted and defended the principle that society serves the individual, not the other way around. It was the rugged individual who tamed the land west of the mountains, fought uncountable odds to survive, and forged a democracy from their labors. "As [the Nation's] horizons expanded, so did [the individual's]," and everyone could be anything they wished, uninhibited by class or other social restrictions. It was the raucous vitality of those stimulated by the newness of the land and the society, not the reasoned judgments of those representing the old social class of the landed gentry, that gave America its spirit and energy.

4. Catton uses the point-by-point structure to develop his essay in paragraphs 4–16, contrasting the generals' backgrounds, philosophies, and the views they embodied as well as comparing their shared personal traits.

5. Catton begins to compare the greatness in each man—the fact that they were both great fighters, had enormous tenacity, were daring and resourceful, and could turn quickly from war to peace.

6. Within paragraphs, Catton tends to move from general to specific, to set up a background or milieu, and then place one general and then the other within it as an outgrowth of his particular background or social circumstance. For example, "Lee was tidewater Virginia . . . A land that was beginning all over again. . . . In such a land . . . was . . . A class of men who lived not to gain advantage for themselves . . . [and] Lee embodied the noblest elements of this aristocratic ideal." Catton not only varies the sentence structure and length to avoid choppiness, he even uses sentence structure to emphasize a point, like the short "individual" sentences in paragraph 8 that are not woven together as tightly as in other paragraphs and thereby "compete" on their own for attention, much like people did on the frontier. Between paragraphs, Catton uses transition words like "yet" and "lastly" as well as repeating words and phrases from previ-

ous material. Paragraph 7, for example, begins "Grant . . . was everything Lee was not."

7. As befits his status as one of our best writers, Catton states his intentions in topic sentences and then delivers what he promises. In paragraph 8, for example, the topic is how the frontier men were opposites of the tidewater aristocrats. Each sentence in the paragraph is unified coherently around the topic, and each has its own mini-contrast around that point. In paragraph 5, each sentence is devoted to describing in ever more detail the tidewater Virginia background of Lee. Catton could perhaps be faulted for not including enough concrete detail, going no further than abstractions like "solemn obligations" or "self-reliant to a fault," but overall, there seems to be enough detail to make the points of contrast between the two men.

8. The advantage of the single sentence in paragraph 3 is that it isolates the thesis and provides a break from the introductory material in paragraph 2. Paragraph 4 is like a headline announcing the beginning of the contrast as well as the key element of the description of both men-an old aristocracy in a new world. In Lee's case, Catton shows how Lee embodied this aristocracy; in Grant's case, Carton highlights how different Grant was from that old aristocratic notion.

9. Catton has a high opinion of both, and the tone is admiring but not fawning. This tone creates an atmosphere that is neither frivolous nor hostile to one side, reflecting, again, Catton's balanced admiration for both these great Americans. The aristocratic South, always easy to criticize as not conducive to democratic ideals and structures, is portrayed by Catton as populated by people meeting "solemn obligations" and looking to its leadership "to give it strength and virtue." Similarly, the individual pioneer was not merely a competitive animal, but one who had a "deep sense of belonging to a national community." The tone of the essay, therefore, comes across as neither argumentative nor merely informative, nor aggressively jingoistic but appropriately serious, thoughtful, and (most important) empathetic to both men who have come to represent two significant regions of the United States.

10. The comparison of both men turning quickly from war to peace suggests the end of the war, the end of their roles as generals, and their final meeting as a paradigm of what the relationship between the North and the South should now be. The end of the essay suggests the scene at the beginning, and as this moment in history ends, so does the essay.

Vocabulary

1. chivalry (5)—social behavior reflecting that idealized by medieval knights, i.e. politeness, honor, self-sacrifice

2. deportment (5)—body language, behavior

3. embodied (6)—an abstraction made concrete

4. tenacity (11)—the quality of holding on for a long time

5. diametrically (12)—totally opposite

6. burgeoning (12)—growing, ballooning

7. indomitable (14)—unbeatable, unable to be dominated

8. reconciliation (16)—the settlement or resolution of a dispute

4. DEFINITION

Discussion

Discussing the clarity with which Lipsitt defines this complex syndrome for a lay reader provides the opportunity to discuss the importance of audience considerations in a definition essay. What words and techniques indicate the targeted audience? Students might research a professional definition of this disease (or *hypochondria*) and compare the two. What are the different purposes? While the reason writers define terms and concepts for lay audiences is rather obvious, professional definitions are necessary for other reasons. Why would a writer define a term for his or her peers? After discussing terms and concepts on which students are the experts, they might practice writing two definitions of one of these terms, one for someone at a similar level as themselves and one for a novice reader.

Answers to Questions

1. The example illustrates the syndrome which Lipsitt will define. A reader will immediately see the intriguing—mystifying—nature of this strange condition.

2. The title indicates a strangeness and puzzling quality to this disease which makes for much more reader interest than a title that would merely suggest a practical definition.

3. Because of the large number of Munchausen patients, the condition accounts for enormous expenses for the health care system, expenses that are usually not reimbursed.

4. Knowing the origin of the name increases the reader's understanding of the fictional nature of the condition and the wandering of the patient from one medical provider to the next. Also, the unusual name might leave a lingering question in the reader's mind if it were not addressed.

5. Without the specific examples a reader could hardly imagine the extremes to which a patient goes to feign illness.

6. The specific patients illustrate the extent to which these individuals persist in their charades. Students might believe an extended example of one particular patient might be even more interesting and instructive.

7. By contrasting Munchausen to hypochondria, Lipsitt refines the definition more distinctly. Munchausen involves not only false illness, but intentional, conscious deception.

8. When Lipsitt explains the causes of Munchausen, he anticipates a typical reader's question, as most would wonder why anyone would try so compulsively to deceive physicians. Also, a full (extended) definition of any disease should include its causes in order to understand its progression.

9. The conclusion is effective because it acknowledges what little is known (and has been explained in the definition) about the syndrome while suggesting there is yet more to learn before its occurrence can be reduced. This conclusion is consistent with his purpose for the definition.

10. Student responses will vary.

Vocabulary

1. fabricates (1)—makes up

2. mimic (2)—imitate

3. incurs (2)—meets with

4. hypochondriacs (4)—persons who believe they are ill

5. sputum (4)—saliva, spit

6. palpably (4)—obviously, easily perceived

7. feasible (4)—reasonable, workable

8. psychoanalytic (7)—pertaining to a method of treating mental disorders by analysis

9. paradoxically (7)—in a seemingly impossible manner

10. odyssey (9)—a long and complicated journey

5. DIVISION AND CLASSIFICATION

"THE PLOT AGAINST PEOPLE"—P. 266

Discussion

As Baker's essay is comic in tone and his purpose is to entertain, class discussion of humor writing is valid here, particularly as many freshman composition students will want to try their hand at comic writing at some point in the course. Ask students if the 1968 publication date limits the effectiveness of Baker's essay in the 1990s. Is it dated in any way? If so, what parts of the essay are dated, and which still seem fresh and effective? Note the importance of word choice. For example, Baker consistently refers to "man" and "mankind." Would this language be considered sexist today? If they were to update Baker's essay, what changes would student writers make? Why?

Answers to Questions

1. Baker's purpose is to entertain his audience by presenting humorous truisms they are likely to empathize with and understand.

2. The thesis statement is the opening sentence of his essay. While students might argue that a more fully developed lead-in would be effective, it should be noted that Baker's direct statement of focus has an appeal of its own as it cuts directly to the essay's subject and provokes the thoughts of the reader.

3. Baker's categories for inanimate objects include "those that don't work, those that break down and those that get lost." He classifies these objects according to behavior—"The method each object uses to achieve its purpose" which is to "resist" and "ultimately defeat" mankind.

4. Baker gives examples to illustrate each category fully and to allow his audience to empathize; readers will recognize the purse that disappears, the furnace that breaks down, and the flashlight that never works. The specifics are a strength of Baker's essay.

5. The category "those that break down" is particularly well developed. Students might cite the example of the automobile (paragraphs 2, 3, and 4). Or, if students

argue that "those that get lost" is particularly vivid, the example of the lost purse might be mentioned (paragraphs 8 and 10).

6. Some examples of personification in the essay include the automobile "with the cunning typical of its breed," the notion that appliances are "in league" to cause maximum frustration for humans, and the idea that "those that don't work" "have truly defeated man by conditioning him never to expect anything of them." This personification is a key part of Baker's humor.

7. Baker's mock-scientific word choice is important to the essay's success (e.g., "Some persons believe this constitutes evidence that inanimate objects are not entirely hostile to man"). A serious essay on this subject is likely to fail because of lack of purpose. Would anyone actually enjoy a factual essay which notes that purses do, indeed, get lost, and automobiles do, in fact, break down?

8. The essay's title reveals the common link between the categories as Baker establishes his "us versus them" comic note.

9. Student responses will vary. Instructors might note that Baker is breaking the traditional composition rule that mandates a minimum of two sentences in a paragraph. The stark finality of Baker's one-sentence conclusion increases the impact of his parting message.

10. Other categories students might mention include inanimate objects that seem harmless when, in fact, they are bent on helping us destroy ourselves (downhill skis, rollerblades, mountain bikes) and inanimate objects that tempt us to make fools of ourselves (microphones, television cameras). These objects, like those in Baker's essay, all help to "defeat" humanity.

Vocabulary

1. inanimate (1)—lifeless, inorganic

2. cunning (3)—craftiness, slyness

3. league (5)—coalition, "in cahoots"

4. evolve (6)—develop, unfold, produce

5. locomotion (7)—movement

6. virtually (9)—practically

7. inherent (10)—essential, innate

8. constitutes (11)—forms, establishes, sets up

9. conciliatory (12)—appeasing, forgiving

10. barometer (13)—instrument that measures atmospheric pressure and helps weather prediction

6. CAUSAL ANALYSIS

Discussion

Explaining human behavior is often just an exercise in speculation. Meyer offers his guess at the reason mysteries appeal to all levels of our society and suggests others are incorrect in believing that the intellectual intrigue of solving the mystery is the real appeal. Some students will see Meyer's point while others may argue against him. If students have not read a number of mysteries, they might consider their reasons for watching mystery movies or television programs. Are they actively, mentally engaged in solving the mystery and is that involvement the reason for their watching? If so, why do people choose to read/watch mysteries to relax? Do students care about the people who are killed or are victims of some misdeed, other than their involvement in the crime? Are television and film characters as "flat" and uncomplicated as Meyer suggests they are in mystery books? Are contemporary mysteries as tidy, as orderly, as Meyer claims? What examples can they think of where a mystery story has brought up serious questions rather than tying up all the loose ends? Students can be encouraged, from this discussion, to see that an effective causal analysis essay can be a very personal view, a very individual attempt to explain why something happens; not all causal analyses are factual and concrete. People often differ when identifying causes and that difference is often what makes such an essay interesting.

Answers to Questions

1. Meyer is trying to explain why people enjoy mysteries.

2. Meyer begins by claiming that people of all types enjoy mysteries. This beginning is effective because the claim leads to the question which drives his essay: Why are all these different people fascinated with mysteries?

3. The author's questions emphasize an apparent contradiction that readers will notice and to which they will possibly object. He is giving voice to questions he knows the reader may have and to which he must provide an answer. These questions lead directly to his thesis.

4. Meyers thesis is that mysteries are "restful" because they are resolved neatly, and that resolution is "reassuring" to a reader whose life is not so simple and easily

organized. The first awareness of this thesis comes in paragraph 7: "A good detective story ties up all the loose ends. . . ."

5. While mysteries have solutions, life often does not. Meyer offers several examples (a plane crash, a flat tire, a missed phone call, an open manhole) from everyday life that seem to can "alter our destiny without rhyme or reason." Once the single problem in the mystery is solved, those involved can go on blithely. In real life, however, people must constantly deal with "chaotic commonplaces."

6. What we are cuddling up to is a very formulaic, organized world which gives us rest from our everyday confusion.

7. Another source of pleasure is watching the "tracking" of the murderer/criminal.

8. While he agrees that readers enjoy watching the "tracking" of the guilty party, he disagrees that their pleasure comes from the intellectual exercise of putting together the pieces of the puzzle created by the writer. He believes readers want to know the resolution, but that they don't work very hard to find it; rather, they are simply pleased when the author presents them with a solution.

9. These casual terms are effective because they are audience oriented. Meyer is writing to those who curl up with the books, not the critics and theorists who analyze them.

10. Meyer concludes that others are wrong; the appeal of mysteries is not their intellectual stimulation but their offering reassurance and vicarious order to a reader. The last sentence effectively and succinctly states the main cause he sets forth.

Vocabulary

1. ubiquitous (1)—ever-present

2. genre (1)—type of literature

3. mayhem (6)—the offense of mutilating or injuring a person

4. anarchic (8)—lawless

5. scrupulously (11)—conscientiously, carefully

6. elitist (12)—one who believes he or she is part of a special or select group

7. pretentious (12)—showy, making claims to importance

8. tenuous (12)—unsubstantial, flimsy

CHAPTER 10: ARGUMENTATION
P. 282

SUMMARY

DEVELOPING YOUR ESSAY
—choose an appropriate title
—know why you hold your views
—anticipate opposing views
—know and remember your audience
—decide which points of argument to include
—organize your essay clearly (patterns A, B, C, and combination)
—argue your ideas logically
—offer evidence that effectively supports your claims
—find the appropriate tone
—consider using Rogerian techniques, if they are appropriate

COMMON LOGICAL FALLACIES
—hasty generalizations
—*non sequitur*
—begging the question
—red herring
—*post hoc, ergo prompter hoc*
—*ad hominem*
—faulty use of authority
—*ad populum*
—circular thinking
—either/or
—hypostatization.
—bandwagon appeal
—straw man
—faulty analogy
—quick fix

Practice, p. 297

ANSWERS TO "PRACTICE" EXERCISES

"Ban Those Books!"—P. 297

Paragraph 1:
　　—argument *ad populum* (use of scare tactics: "very existence . . . is threatened")
　　—either/or fallacy ("cleanse . . . or reconcile ourselves")

Paragraph 2:
　　—hypostatization ("History has shown")
　　—begging the question ("immoral books," "Communist plot")
　　—argument *ad populum* ("liberal free-thinkers and radicals" are threatening names to some people)
　　—*post hoc* (the number of cut classes and the decline in the number of seniors going on to college were not necessarily caused by placing the books in the library that year)

Paragraph 3:
　　—either/or fallacy ("natural decline . . . or the influence of those dirty books")
　　—*non sequitur* (obviously, other reasons can exist for the changes in the students' behavior)
　　—begging the question ("dirty books," "undesirable characters")
　　—argument *ad populum* ("innocent children")

Paragraph 4:
　　—argument *ad populum* ("simple man . . . farm boy" versus the "pseudointellectuals," "Communist conspiracy," "good folks")
　　—bandwagon appeal (all the "right-thinking neighbors")

DISCUSSION, ANSWERS TO QUESTIONS, VOCABULARY

Discussion

Consider dividing your class into two teams and have them debate this subject prior to reading the two essays. By debating the issue beforehand, they will bring their own perspectives to the articles, perhaps seeing more clearly the strengths and weaknesses of each piece. After the essays are read, have students choose the essay they each found more persuasive. Remind them that a key part of objectivity in this judgment is separating their own beliefs from those presented. In other words, they should not be tempted automatically to pick the essay they agree with as the stronger of the two.

Answers to Questions

1. *USA TODAY* argues against social promotion because it is ineffective. The editor not only criticizes the practice but offers a solution to the problem.

2. The editorial suggests social promotion is negative because it may, in fact, cause more problems for students as they attempt the next sequence of classes if they have not passed the earlier levels. It also argues that failing students is a simplistic solution, that telling students "Sorry. Try again," will not increase either their skill or motivation level. The editorial claims that refusing to pass students who fail to accomplish established objectives will teach them that achievement is worthwhile, that "competence counts."

3. Several opposing arguments are addressed: 1) retained students will lose self-esteem, 2) research has not shown that students repeating a class improve their outcomes, 3) students who are held back drop out at drastically increasing rates, and 4) special programs to address the problem will be expensive. By bringing up these opposition points, the writer demonstrates a more full understanding of the problem and takes possible readers' opinions into consideration.

4. The editorial suggests that the problem is not an all or nothing argument and that other interventions can address non-achieving students. The specific examples are given to illustrate successful programs which have identified problem learners and have helped them work on their skills. By acknowledging that special programs will be costly, the writer addresses a question that is sure to be raised in the reader's mind. The writer also makes sure to resolve the issue for the reader by reasoning that special programs would certainly not be more expensive than paying for an entire year of repeated schooling.

5. One of the strengths of this argument is its reasonable approach—it discusses the complexity of the problem. The initial argument that each year builds on the previous ones and that social promotion ignores that process is certainly a strong point, although somewhat underdeveloped in this essay. Students may cite paragraphs 5 and 7 as a particularly strong since they use some concrete evidence rather than just assertions in their development. Some may feel the writer's claim that the self-esteem theory is mistaken is undermined later in the essay; if 20-30% more retained students drop out, it may have something to do with their self-esteem.

6. Neill does not believe that test-based promotion is the answer to non-achieving. He cites many reasons for his claim: 1) testing professionals say that tests should not be the only measure of achievement because tests are imprecise measurements, 2) research indicates students who are held back will still be at the

bottom of the class when promoted the next year, 3) students who are not promoted are more inclined to drop out, 4) repeating grades is expensive for the taxpayer, and 5) promotion based on testing encourages "test coaching."

7. Students who are retained still do not achieve satisfactorily and they are more inclined to drop out.

8. Teaching to a test can focus on rote memorization which, says Neill, is one of the reasons students dislike school. Test coaching also deprives students of "many important things" since curriculum is often pared down to only tested material.

9. Neill's best argument is for the invalidity of testing as an accurate standard for passing or failing a grade. This argument is developed much more fully than the others, although students may question the appropriateness and applicability of the specific example of SAT scores to an argument primarily about grade school. The other arguments, though they appear reasonable, have little evidence to convince a reader.

10. Student responses will vary, although many will see the fairness and thoroughness of the first to be more convincing.

Vocabulary

USA Today's editorial:
  1. sequential (2)—following in a regular series

  2. mediocrity (3)—ordinary or middle quality

  3. absolving (3)—freeing from an obligation

  4. scant (5)—little, small amount

  5. competence (9)—adequate ability

M. Neill's response:
  1. retention (2)—holding back

  2. imprecision (4)—lack of exactness

  3. fostered (6)—encouraged, stimulated

DISCUSSION OF PRO/CON ADVERTISEMENTS, P. 309

Student responses to these advertisements will vary. Instructors might use discussion of these advertisements to emphasize that one's personal beliefs about gun-control and the safe use of energy should not make the reader blind to the various appeals—both effective and flawed—that the advertisements employ. Some of the appeals used are listed below.

N.R.A. advertisement: gives biographical details that present Gutman as a successful business and civic leader and family-oriented man: emphasizes his experiences in communist Cuba and the Florida legislature to add authority to his support for the N.R.A., thus perhaps strengthening the credibility of the N.R.A. for the reader.

Center to Prevent Handgun Violence advertisement: emphasizes the contrast between "self-styled 'citizen militias'" which cite the Second Amendment as support for their weapons and military training, and the National Guard, which the ad states is the true militia protected by the Second Amendment (the photo of the militia group plays on reader emotions); Supreme Court Justice Warren Burger's views are quoted (appealing to reader's regard for intellectual authority) to strengthen the advertisement's claim that the Second Amendment does not prohibit gun-control laws.

U.S. Council for Energy Awareness advertisement: a largely emotional appeal centered around the photo of a baby sea turtle; emphasizes the environmental safety of nuclear energy by implying that is has less negative impact on endangered species and fragile ecosystems other than energy sources.

Metropolitan Energy Council, Inc. advertisement: an emotional appeal emphasizing the danger of gas heat (a mother and her toddler are pictured); the advertisement insinuates that gas utilities are uncaring and perhaps even negligent toward public safety.

CHAPTER 11: DESCRIPTION
P. 315

SUMMARY

HOW TO WRITE EFFECTIVE DESCRIPTION
    —recognize your purpose
    —describe clearly, using specific details
    —select only appropriate details
    —make your descriptions vivid
Problems to Avoid:
    —remember your audience
    —avoid an erratic organization of details
    —avoid any sudden change in perspective

DISCUSSION, ANSWERS TO QUESTIONS, VOCABULARY

"THE DISCUS THROWER"—P. 327

Discussion

Most students find this to be a strange, even haunting essay. The atmosphere has overtones of a haunted house and tortured souls within. The point of view as an observer is especially well chosen, for we feel we are observing the secret, inner life of another human being and are rather excited at the prospect. The imagery is rich, and puts into practice most of the suggestions about good description mentioned in the chapter previously. Readers are especially drawn in because the actions of the patient are so enigmatic—so out of context for the hospital—that their very strangeness compels the reader to "picture" not only the overt physical situation, but also the very mind and heart of the patient. As such, it is a potent piece of writing because it touches those deep emotional issues in all of us.

Answers to Questions

1. The point of view is from the doctor, one of those rare types who likes to spy on his patients to see the actual results of his ministrations or just get to know the patient a little better. It is introduced in the short, almost whimsical first sentence.

2. The essay contains both kinds of description, and there are just enough details to keep the reader interested and on the track of the writer's intentions. Selzer's descriptions of the "rusted," not "tanned," skin, the body like a "rotting log," and the process of cleaning the stumps all combine to make the total "discus thrower" image alive.

3. The description of the room—"empty of all possessions"—reveals the isolation of the patient. He is alone in his battle against death.

4. Selzer's title is ironic because the Greek athlete is the essence of fitness and vigor, not at all the patient's condition. The patient is fighting his deteriorated state in any way still available, by anger and defiance (throwing the eggs) and by denial (calling for shoes).

5. He is empathetic. His curiosity is enough to make us think this—his coming back repeatedly to observe not a medical condition but his patient's state of mind. Also, the questions he asks the staff indicate his concern. The attitude of the head nurse is that there is no excuse for uncivil behavior, no matter how sick you are.

6. Seltzer is describing a universal human condition as exemplified by a representative human being. He doesn't do anything to contain the patient's expression of his individuality because 1) that's not his job and 2) he has already done for him medically what he can.

7. —like the windows of a snowbound cottage
   —the look of a bonsai, roots and branches pruned into the dwarfed facsimile of
      a great tree
   —of when his body was not a rotting log
   —as though he were a sailor standing athwart a slanting deck

8. Dialogue varies the tone, pace, and syntax of the essay. It also allows another point of view to be presented.

9. The clean wall is an effective ending since it implies emptiness, a sense of loss, and the passing of an interesting and valuable human being.

10. The patient never gives up, never relinquishes his right to live as an individual and his right to rage against dying and the unfairness of fate and the world.

Vocabulary

1. furtive (1)—secret, stealthy

2. vile (2)—horrible

3. repose (2)—lying down to rest

4. facsimile (2)—copy

5. caches (4)—hidden or secret stores

6. kickshaws (4)—trinkets

7. shard (19)—broken piece of pottery

8. inert (20)—inactive

9. athwart (20)—across

10. irony (23)—use of words or actions to convey the opposite of their literal meaning

CHAPTER 12: NARRATION
P. 333

SUMMARY

EXTENDED VERSUS BRIEF NARRATIVES

HOW TO WRITE EFFECTIVE NARRATION
—know your purpose
—make your main point clear
—follow a logical time sequence
—use details to present the setting
—make your characters believable
—use dialogue realistically

Problems to Avoid:
-choose your subject carefully
-limit your scope
-don't let your story lag with insignificant detail

DISCUSSION, ANSWERS TO QUESTIONS, VOCABULARY

"SISTER FLOWERS"—P. 342

Discussion

Students might be encouraged to examine Angelou's narrative from two standpoints: her use of description, which allows her readers to see Sister Flowers and the essay's setting, and her use of dialogue, which allows her readers to hear key conversations. Why are both components necessary to present a fully rounded portrait of time, character, and place? A discussion of Angelou's use of specific and sensory details will enable students to examine ways to fully re-create scenes in their own narrative essays. Students may be interested to know that following the sexual abuse by her mother's husband, Angelou was mute for much of her childhood prior to meeting Mrs. Flowers.

Answers to Questions

1. Angelou's main purpose is to show how Sister Flowers brought more than a love of language to her; Sister Flowers gave Angelou a sense of dignity and refinement she longed for.

2. The images Angelou uses to describe Sister Flowers set her apart from the rest of Stamps. The "private breeze" that surrounded her made her appear cool when the rest of the population was sweltering. In the description of Sister Flowers's appearance, the details again set her apart, contrasting hers to the more typical farmer's appearance. Angelou's comparison of Sister Flowers's skin to the skin of a plum builds the image of delicacy and elegance. Although the reader knows Sister Flowers is "our side's answer to the richest white woman in town," Angelou tempers this image with a description of her genuine and warm smile.

3. Angelou sets up the reader for a later irony by having Momma speak to Sister Flowers in nonstandard English, by which Angelou is embarrassed. This early embarrassment is important because Sister Flowers makes a point of telling the young Angelou she should be tolerant of illiteracy.

4. As an adult, Angelou can see the relationship of mutual respect between her grandmother and Sister Flowers that reached across the educational differences.

5. Angelou was impressed by Mrs. Flowers because she was the closest thing in her culture to the elegant women in the literature Angelou read. She is compared to the heroines of novels. Angelou is glad never to have heard white people demean Sister Flowers because she would not want anything to tarnish this image of refinement and gentility.

6. Angelou was a very bright young girl who read constantly; the reader knows this from the many allusions to heroines of novels as well as the young Angelou's thoughts of Beowulf and Oliver Twist. Mrs. Flowers knows of her reading and also lets the reader know of Angelou's fine school work.

7. The extraordinary things about Sister Flowers's house—the ice on an ordinary day, white, fresh curtains and a cookie plate covered with a tea towel—continued to set Mrs. Flowers apart from Angelou's existence. The cookies and lemonade were of crucial importance because they were made especially for Angelou and made her feel valued.

8. Dialogue is important to this section of the story because it is the sound of language that becomes so compelling to Angelou through Mrs. Flowers's reading. The words that Angelou utters after listening, spellbound, to Mrs. Flowers are the first she has uttered in a long time and they are more powerful in dialogue form.

9. Angelou's descriptive detail is complete and gives vivid pictures for the reader of places and people. Students may cite dialogue as important detail and also cite the vivid visual detail related to Mrs. Flowers and her home. Also, Angelou gives details of the feelings she was having throughout the experience. The reader understands her anxiety over what to wear, her attempt to use her best manners, her excitement over hearing the words of *A Tale of Two Cities* spoken as poetry, etc.

10. Many times a writer has understandings about his or her narrative that are implied by the story, but not fully explained. Frequently it is a good idea to share those understandings with the reader and not to take for granted that the reader will be on the same wavelength. The importance of making a traumatized and insecure young girl feel special is emphasized in these paragraphs. These last paragraphs also add the perspective of adult reflection to that of the young girl in the story.

Vocabulary

1. voile (2)—a thin, sheer fabric

2. benign (4)—well meaning

3. gait (8)—manner of walking

4. morocco-bound (11)—covered in a fine, textured leather

5. chifforobe (17)—a narrow, high chest of drawers

6. infuse (24)—to put in, as by pouring

7. boggled (27)—overwhelmed by complexity

8. leered (32)—a sly, sidelong took displaying ill will

9. homely (35)—simple, crude, ordinary

10. aura (42)—an invisible atmosphere supposedly surrounding a person or thing

11. wormwood (42)—a bitter oil used in making absinthe; therefore, a bitter, unpleasant, or mortifying experience

12. mead (42)—an alcoholic ale

Chapter 13: Writing Essays Using Multiple Strategies
p. 349

SUMMARY

COMBINING STRATEGIES
— strategies are seldom used in isolation
— strategies are various ways to think about a topic
— strategies serve a specific purpose

CHOOSING THE BEST STRATEGIES
— questions to help select strategies to match your purpose
Problems to Avoid

DISCUSSION, ANSWERS TO QUESTIONS, VOCABULARY

I. EXAMPLE

"DON'T LET STEREOTYPES WARP YOUR JUDGMENTS"—P. 356

Discussion

Students can readily identify with this essay by listing on the board a variety of stereo-types they have experienced either by having judged, or by having been judged by, others. If they were going to write a similar essay or respond to this one, what specific examples from their experience could they offer? After this discussion, use question #10 below (identifying the different strategies Heilbroner uses) as the basis for a group activity. Divide students into groups and have them list the strategies in the essay and why the author has used each at a specific point in the essay. Each group can explain a few paragraphs in a feedback session after this group work. After reading this essay, the class might reflect on (or read, if they haven't already) "Black Men in Public Space," by Brent Staples (Additional Readings, p. 497). How does Heilbroner's essay relate to Staples's experience?

Answers to Questions

1. Heilbroner uses these questions to call up common stereotypes most readers will

share in order to connect readers to the practice of pre-judging people. If he were to begin differently, with a definition of prejudice, for example, readers might immediately react that they certainly are not prejudiced. The examples will help readers see they all share some of these sometimes subtle stereotypes.

2. Heilbroner defines a stereotype as "a kind of gossip about the world" which is the basis of prejudice. The studies illustrate that stereotyping is a sub-conscious, ever-present influence on our perceptions and beliefs.

3. Using first person includes Heilbroner in "those who stereotype" and, by this admission, connects him more closely to the readers who are also a part of "we." By doing so, the essay becomes more of an easily accepted observation on a tendency of human nature rather than a scolding lecture such as "You should not pre-judge others."

4. One of the reasons stereotypes develop is that as children we begin "type casting" people, sorting out the "good guys" and the "bad guys." Also, the media perpetuates stereotypes in jokes, characterizations, and advertising. We stereotype to make sense of the confusion of our world, to give definition to the chaos around us.

5. One who stereotypes loses the opportunity to create an individual picture of the world. By seeing the world as so many categories of identical "cutouts" instead of seeing it as diverse and nuanced, the person becomes a stereotype who is totally predictable and inflexible.

6. Heilbroner's opening examples are hypothetical (see answer #1 above). The specific examples from the studies add concrete support to his claim about the ubiquitous nature of stereotyping. In paragraph 11, the author cites two commonly held stereotypes to explain how we rationalize and confirm our prejudices. Other groups of frequently held stereotypes found in paragraphs 12 and 15 help a reader begin to recognize and question those beliefs.

7. The three step process in paragraphs 18-20 outlines a way readers can acknowledge complexity and individuality rather than perpetuate stereotypes.

8. These quotations lend authority and a broader perspective than just Heilbroner's to his opinions.

9. The conclusion underscores what the reader has to gain from the essay. The metaphor of paintings in a gallery is a memorable way for the reader to go away with a strong grasp of the overall process of stereotyping; the metaphor condenses the process into a vivid mental picture.

10. Strategies used in the essay:

    Paragraphs 1 - 3   Hypothetical examples
    Paragraph 4   Specific examples
    Paragraph 5   Definition
    Paragraph 6   Specific examples
    Paragraphs 7 - 13   Causal analysis
    Paragraphs 15 - 19   Process analysis

Vocabulary

1. swarthy (4)—dark complexioned

2. dinned (8)—told repeatedly and persistently

3. perpetuated (8)—continued indefinitely

4. synchronized (9)—regulated the timing of

5. semantics (11)—study of the relationship between words and their meanings

6. vindicated (11)—cleared from suspicion or guilt

7. impoverish (12)—to make poor

8. chastening (18)—correcting by punishment

9. edifice (18)—an imposing building

10. chary (19)—shy, cautious

Part Three

Special Assignments

CHAPTER 14: WRITING A PAPER USING RESEARCH
P. 365

SUMMARY

FOCUSING YOUR TOPIC
—some are assigned and already specific and narrowed
—others are more general and need a little or a lot of narrowing

BEGINNING YOUR LIBRARY RESEARCH
—computer catalogs/the card catalog
—periodical indexes
—electronic sources
—special collections

PREPARING A WORKING BIBLIOGRAPHY

CHOOSING AND EVALUATING YOUR SOURCES

The writer should ask:
—What do I know about the author?
—What do I know about the publisher?
—Is my research reasonably balanced?
—Are my sources reporting valid research?
—Are my sources still current?

PREPARING AN ANNOTATED BIBLIOGRAPHY

[Note: Requiring students to compile an annotated bibliography at this stage of the research process may be an effective way of assuring progress is being made. This might help writers avoid the weak research sources so often found in a frenzied last minute search.]

TAKING NOTES
   —content and bibliographic cards
   —direct quotations
   —paraphrase
   —summary
   —your own ideas

INCORPORATING YOUR SOURCE MATERIAL
   —use your sources in a clear, logical way
   —don't overuse direct quotations
   —don't "drop in" direct quotations next to your prose
   —vary your sentence pattern when you present quotations
   —punctuate your quotations correctly
   —make certain your support is in your paper
   —don't let reference material dominate your essay

AVOIDING PLAGIARISM

Practice, p. 383

CHOOSING THE DOCUMENTATION STYLE FOR YOUR ESSAY

[Jean Wyrick would like readers to know that as this edition of *Steps* went to press, the MLA was making new decisions about the documentation of electronic sources, most particularly internet sources. She chose to use the most current suggestions available, knowing that, in this rapidly changing electronic environment, you who deal with student questions and electronic formats on a daily basis will be able to supply ongoing updates to the text. She apologizes for that complication and any corrosponding changes you will have to make to the text's explanations and examples, but knows you understand the difficulty.]

A. MLA Style
   —parenthetical reference form
   —compiling a Works Cited List
   —sample entries: MLA Style

B. Footnote/Bibliography Form

C. APA Style

USING SUPPLEMENTARY NOTES

ANSWERS TO "PRACTICE" EXERCISES

[Users of previous editions should notice that hte research in Amy Lawrence's paper has been updated. At the time of publicaiton, all bodies were accounted for with the exception of one daughter; there is still controversy over which daughter is missing.]

Practice, p. 383

1. Bibliography Card

   Brun, Geoffrey and Ferguson, Wallace K. <u>A Survey of European Civilization Part Two, Since 1660.</u> Boston: Houghton Mifflin Company, 1962. Notes from p. 716.

2. Paraphrase

   Alexander got the title of "Tsar liberator" by freeing 40 million Russian serfs. Rural Russia in the early 1800s was very medieval. Less than 100,000 of the nobility held more than nine-tenths of the land. Serfs could be sold, forced to be servants, or sent to factories for the master's own profit. Though some nobles were like kindly fathers to their "children," others overworked their serfs, beat them, and invaded their privacy whenever they wanted. A serf could not get married or leave the estate without permission and would be chased, dragged back, and punished if he did. Basically, a serf was at the mercy of his master.

3. Summary

   Alexander was the tsar who freed 40 million Russian serfs. Russia in the early nineteenth century was very medieval in that a minority of noble families held most of the land. Serfs could be sold, told to be servants, or sent to work in factories. Some nobles were good to their serfs, but others abused them. A serf had no rights and could be punished for disobeying his master.

4. In their survey of European civilization, Brun and Ferguson point out that some serfs were "sent to the factories in the towns for their master's profit" (716).

5. Nineteenth-century Russia was still an undemocratic country. Not only was most of the land held by a minority of the nobility, but as Brun and Ferguson note, the peasants (serfs) had no rights and could even "be sold with the estates to new landlords" (716).

CHAPTER 15: WRITING ABOUT LITERATURE
P. 407

SUMMARY

USING LITERATURE IN THE COMPOSITION CLASSROOM
— prompts: using literature as a springboard for an essay
— literary analysis: interpretation of a piece of literature

STEPS TO READING STORIES
— check bibliographical information
— read story once for plot
— look up important vocabulary words
— make preliminary notes on major themes
— analyze story's parts and reason for each; evaluate point of view
— analyze structure of story
— analyze characters
— examine setting and its import
— study language use: figurative language, symbols, style, and tone
— review and refine initial reactions

STEPS TO READING A POEM
— check bibliographical information
— read poem at least twice, paraphrase poem, analyze sentences and vocabulary
— decide if poem is narrative or lyrical; determine dominate idea
— analyze narrator of poem
— examine the setting or occasion of poem
— analyze characters
— examine the poem's word choice
— analyze the structure of the poem
— examine the sound devices

SOME GUIDELINES FOR WRITING AN ESSAY ABOUT LITERATURE
— select a workable topic
— present a clear thesis
— follow literary conventions
— organize effectively
— use ample evidence
— find a pleasing conclusion

Practice, p. 429

Problems to avoid

ANSWERS TO "PRACTICE" EXERCISE

Practice, p. 429

1. Since Robinson was interested in human psychology, students can speculate before reading that this poem may focus on the characters' psychological states.

2. After reading, students may need to look up *imperially*; the sentence structure is straightforward.

3. "Richard Cory" is a narrative poem since it tells a story.

4. The narrators are working class people who are jealous of Cory because he seems to have and be everything they desire. They don't understand what private despair he must be experiencing

5. The setting is contemporary to Robinson's time; it was written approximately 100 years ago. The working class narrators would have had very difficult lives while Cory never had to work; he was a member of the wealthy upper class who, at that time, spent their lives in social and cultural pursuits.

6. Cory contrasts distinctly with his observers, the narrators. While they know him, he is not at all involved in their world. The jealousy they feel toward him abruptly changes when they realize his life is not as blessed as they had perceived.

7. The poem's diction is simple, as would be the townspeople's. The language is literal, not figurative, for the most part. However, the phrase "waited for the light" has a double meaning. The working people were both waiting for literal light as they worked in the early morning and late night and were waiting for some enlightenment, some deliverance from their miserable lives.

8. The poem is a fixed form composed of four-line stanzas.

9. The poem is written in quatrains, the end rhyme pattern being abab, dcdc, efef, ghgh.

10. Except for line 4, which varies slightly, Robinson's lines are iambic pentameter—five sets (feet) of syllables, each with an unaccented syllable followed by an accented syllable.

CHAPTER 16: WRITING IN-CLASS ASSIGNMENTS
P. 431

SUMMARY

STEPS TO WRITING WELL UNDER PRESSURE
A. Clarify for yourself the kind of task you face.
   —"short answer" exam questions
   —essay exam questions
   —personal opinion essays
   —summary-and-response essays
B. Read the assignment with great care.
C. Prepare to write.
   —think positively
   —take the first few minutes to think and plan
   —after choosing a thesis jot down a brief plan or outline
   —budget your time before beginning to write
D. Begin writing, remembering what you have learned about paragraphing, topic sentences, and supporting evidence.
   —write on only one side of the paper
   —try to conclude your essay in a satisfactory way
E. If time allows, read what you have written.
   —be sure your name is on your essay
Problems to Avoid:
   —misreading the assignment
   —incomplete essay/exam
   —composition amnesia
   —gorilla generalizations

Practice, p. 438

ANSWERS TO "PRACTICE" EXERCISES

Practice, p. 438.
A. 1. Underline "flower imagery" and "major theme . . . The Bluest Eye. Circle "Discuss," "examples," and "clarify."

   2. Underline "the Bay of Pigs . . . Cuba." Circle "Trace" and "the events that led to."

3. Underline "Louis B. Mayer" and "American Film . . . of Moviemaking." Circle "Discuss" and "major influences on."

4. Underline "The 1957 . . . system. Circle "Agree or disagree."

5. Underline "the surrealistic . . . Dali" and "important . . . artists. Circle "Consider the similarities . . . between" and "Illustrate . . . references to."

B. Student responses will vary.

PART FOUR
A CONCISE HANDBOOK

CHAPTER 17: MAJOR ERRORS IN GRAMMAR
P. 443

SUMMARY

ERRORS WITH VERBS
—faulty agreement
—subjunctive
—tense shift
—split infinitive
—double negatives
—passive voice

Practice, p. 448

ERRORS WITH NOUNS
—possessive with "-ing" nouns
—misuse of nouns as adjectives

ERRORS WITH PRONOUNS
—faulty agreement
—vague reference
—shift in pronouns
—incorrect case

Practice, p. 453

ERRORS WITH ADVERBS AND ADJECTIVES
—incorrect usage
—faulty comparison

ERRORS IN MODIFYING PHRASES
—dangling modifiers
—misplaced modifiers

Practice, p. 456

ERRORS IN SENTENCES
    —fragments
    —comma splice
    —run-on sentence
    —faulty parallelism
    —false predication
    —mixed structure
Practice, pp. 458, 459, 462

ANSWERS TO "PRACTICE" EXERCISES

Practice, p. 448

A. 1. A recent report on Cuban land crabs <u>shows</u> they can run faster than horses.

2. The team from Snooker Hollow High School <u>is</u> considering switching from basketball to basket weaving because passing athletics is now required for graduation.

3. None of the students <u>knows</u> that both mystery writer Agatha Christie and inventor Thomas Edison <u>were</u> dyslexic.

4. Each of the twins <u>has</u> read about Joseph Priestley's contribution to the understanding of oxygen, but neither <u>was</u> aware that he also invented the pencil eraser.

5. Clarity in speech and writing <u>is</u> absolutely essential in the business world today.

6. Some scholars believe that the world's first money, in the form of coins, <u>was</u> made in Lydia, a country that is now part of Turkey.

7. Bananas, rich in vitamins and low in fats, <u>are</u> rated the most popular fruit in America.

8. There <u>are</u> many children in this country who appreciate a big plate of hot grits, but none of the Hall children <u>likes</u> this Southern dish.

9. Either the cocker spaniel or the poodle <u>holds</u> the honor of being the most popular breed of dogs in the United States, <u>says</u> the American Kennel Club.

10. Many people <u>consider</u> Johnny Appleseed a mythical figure, but now two

local historians, authors of a well-known book on the subject, <u>argue</u> he was a real person named John Chapman.

B. 1. She could hardly wait to hear Johnny Cash sing his version of her favorite song, "I've Been Flushed from the Bathroom of Your Heart."

2. "If you were in Wyoming and couldn't hear the wind blowing, what would people call you?" asked Jethro. "Dead," replied his buddy Herman.

3. The Aztec ruler Montezuma believed that chocolate had magical powers and could act as an aphrodisiac.

4. Tammy's favorite band is Opie Gone Bad, so she always buys their new album every six months or so.

5. The Fire Department is raising suspicions of arson following the burning of the new Chip and Dale Furniture Factory. (Or, "Following the burning of the new Chip and Dale Furniture Factory, the Fire Department is raising suspicions of arson.")

Practice, p. 453

1. The executive knew she was in trouble when her salary was <u>cut in half.</u>

2. Correct.

3. It was a surprise to both Mary and <u>me</u> to learn that Switzerland didn't give women the right to vote until 1971.

4. Each of the young women in the Family Life class decided not to marry after <u>she</u> read that couples today have 2.3 children.

5. Jim Bob explained that the best way for Frankie to avoid recurring nosebleeds was to stay out of <u>Jim Bob's</u> marital arguments.

6. Those of us who'd had the flu agreed that <u>we</u> could always get <u>our</u> doctor to return <u>our</u> calls quicker if <u>we</u> got in the shower.

7. The stranger gave the free movie tickets to Louise and <u>me</u> after he saw people standing in line to leave the theater.

8. The personnel director told each of the employees, most of <u>whom</u> opposed him, to signify <u>his</u> or <u>her</u> "no" vote by saying, "I resign."

9. Clarence and <u>I</u> have an uncle who is so mean he writes the name of the murderer on the first page of mystery novels that are passed around the family.

10. The first movie to gross over one million dollars was <u>Tarzan of the Apes</u> (1932) starring Johnny Weissmuller, a former Olympic star who became an actor. <u>Such a large profit</u> was unusual in the movie industry at that time. (Or: At that time, it was unusual for Olympic champions to become movie stars.)

Practice, p. 456

1. Squeezing the can, I still found it hard to tell if the tomatoes were ripe.

2. Although liver is probably the worst food in the world, buttermilk is hardly any better.

3. After the optometrist pulled her eye tooth, Hortense didn't behave very well in the waiting room.

4. Because the car was eight years old, he didn't think it would make it over the mountains.

5. Since they were so rich, the James brothers decided to have their cattle engraved instead of branded.

6. In the first race of the Death Valley Swim Meet, Maria could use the backstroke or sidestroke, whichever was better for her.

7. I didn't do well on my nature project because my bonsai sequoia tree grew poorly in its small container.

8. After boarding Hard Luck Airways, we were offered meals that convinced us to return by ship.

9. In a book from the public library I've read that a number of modern sailors, like Thor Heyerdahl, have sailed primitive vessels across the ocean.

10. To help you call the fire department, we are enclosing in this letter a new telephone number that may be attached to your telephone.

Practice, p. 458

1. According to Lawrence M. Ausbel, author of "Credit Cards" in *The McGraw-Hill Encyclopedia of Economics,* the idea of a credit card first appeared in 1887.

2. Originally an imaginary concept in a futurist novel by Edward Bellamy, the card allowed characters to charge against future earnings.

3. Around the turn of the century some American stores issued paper or metal "shoppers' plates," although they were only used by retailers to identify their credit customers.

4. The first real credit card was issued in 1947 by a New York bank and was a success despite the fact that customers could only charge purchases in a two-block area in Brooklyn.

5. Travel and entertainment cards soon appeared, including the American Express card in 1958 and Carte Blanche in 1959, that allowed customers to charge items and services across the country.

Practice, p. 459

1. My mother is very politically conservative; she's written in George III for president in the last two elections.

2. Mary Lou decided not to eat the alphabet soup because the letters spelled out "botulism."

3. A friend of mine offers a good definition of nasty theater critics on opening night. According to him, they're the people who can't wait to stone the first cast.

4. Opportunists who came to the South after the Civil War were often called "carpetbaggers" since they carried their belongings in cheaply produced travel bags made of Belgian carpet.

5. A dried gourd containing seeds probably functioned as the first baby rattle. Ancient Egyptian wall paintings show babies with such gourds clutched in their fingers.

6. The Smithsonian Institute was started when English scientist James Smithson died in 1829 and willed his entire fortune to the United States to establish a foundation for knowledge.

7. The word "jack-o'-lantern" may have come from the legend of Irish Jack. A mean old man in life, he was condemned after death to wander the earth carrying a hollow turnip with a lump of burning coal inside.

8. Americans forget how large the blue whale is. It has a heart as large as a Volkswagen Beetle and can hold an elephant on its tongue.

9. Correct.

10. The famous Eiffel Tower, built for the 1889 Paris Exposition has inspired many crazy stunts: in 1891, Silvain Domon climbed the 363 steps on stilts.

Practice, p. 462

1. Is it true that Superman could leap tall buildings, run faster than a locomotive, and deflect bullets with his skin?

2. He proved his intelligence by bringing home a twenty-pound block of ice after ice fishing all day.

3. We attended the Texas Spamarama Festival to participate in the spambalaya cook-off, the spam-can toss, the spam jam jazz session, and the dancing to such favorites as "Twist and Snout."

4. My Aunt Clara swears she has seen Elvis snacking at the deli, browsing at the supermarket, munching at the pizza parlor, and reading in the cook book section of a local book store.

5. According to my husband, summer air in Louisiana is one part oxygen, nine parts water, and ninety percent mosquitos.

CHAPTER 18: A CONCISE GUIDE TO PUNCTUATION
P. 463

SUMMARY

THE PERIOD

THE QUESTION MARK

THE EXCLAMATION POINT

THE COMMA
Practice, p. 469

THE SEMICOLON

THE COLON
Practice, p. 472

THE APOSTROPHE

QUOTATION MARKS
Practice, p. 472

PARENTHESES

BRACKETS

THE DASH

THE HYPHEN

UNDERLINING

THE ELLIPSIS MARK
Practice, p. 476
Practice, p. 483

ANSWERS TO "PRACTICE" EXERCISES

Practice, p. 469

A. 1. In 1886 temperance leader Harvey Wilcox left Kansas and purchased 120 acres near Los Angeles to develop a new town.

2. Although there were no holly trees growing in that part of California, Mrs. Wilcox named the area Hollywood.

3. Mrs. Wilcox may have named the place after a friend's summer home located in Illinois.

4. During the early years, settlers who shared the Wilcoxs' values moved to the area and banned the recreational drinking of alcoholic beverages. However, some alcohol consumption was allowed for medicinal purposes.

5. Nevertheless, by 1910 the first film studio opened its doors inside a tavern on Sunset Boulevard. Within seven short years, the quiet community started by the Wilcoxs had vanished.

B. 1. Yes, Hortense, in the 1920s young women did indeed cut their hair, raise their hemlines, dab perfume behind their knees, and dance the Charleston.

2. In 1873 Cornell University canceled the school's first intercollegiate football game with Michigan when the president announced, "I will not permit 30 men to travel 400 miles merely to agitate a bag of wind."

3. Jane, Marian, Donna, Ann, and Cissy graduated from high school on June 5, 1964, in Texarkana, Texas, in the old Walnut Street Auditorium.

4. "I may be a man of few opinions," said Henry, "but I insist that I am neither for nor against apathy."

5. Did you know, for instance, that early American settlers once thought the tomato was so poisonous they only used the plant for decoration?

C. 1. The father decided to recapture his youth. He took his son's car keys away.

2. Although ice cream didn't appear in America until the 1700s, our country now leads the world in ice cream consumption. Australia is second, I think.

3. Last summer the large, friendly family that fives next door flew Discount Airlines and visited three cities on their vacation. However, their suitcases visited five.

4. Researchers in Balboa, Panama, have discovered that the poisonous, yellow-belly sea snake, which descended from the cobra, is the most deadly serpent in the world.

5. Lulu Belle, my cousin, spent the week of September 1–7, 1986, in the Woods near Dimebox, Texas, looking for additions to her extinct butterfly collection. However, she wasn't at all successful in her search.

Practice, p. 472

1. My doctor failed in his career as a kidnapper; no one could read his ransom notes.

2. Some of the cars manufactured between 1907 and 1912 that didn't achieve the popularity of the Model T were the Black Crow, the Swallow, the Bugmobile, and the Carnation.

3. The highest point in the United States is Mt. McKinley at 20,320 feet; in contrast, the lowest point is Death Valley at 282 feet below sea level.

4. There's only one thing that can make our lawn look as good as our neighbor's: snow.

5. In a Thurmont, Maryland, cemetery can be found this epitaph: "Here lies an Atheist, all dressed up, and no place to go."

6. According to an 1863 book of etiquette, the perfect hostess will see to it that the works of male and female authors are properly separated on her bookshelves; however, if the authors happen to be married, their proximity may be tolerated.

7. Some inventors who named weapons after themselves include Samuel Colt, the Colt revolver; Henry Deringer, Jr., the derringer [sic] pistol; Dr. Richard J. Gatling, the crank machine gun; Col. John T. Thompson, the submachine or "tommy" gun; and Oliver F. Winchester, the repeating rifle. (Or: include these:)

8. Correct.

9. As we drove down the highway we saw a sign that said, "See the World's Largest Prairie Dog; Turn Right at this Exit." Therefore we stopped to look.

10. The next billboard read, "See Live Rattlesnakes; Pet Baby Pigs," making us want to stop again.

Practice, p. 476

A. 1. A horse's pajamas

2. The queen's throne

3. The tree lost its leaves

4. Ten students' grades

5. The Depression of the 1930's (or 1930s)

6. That dress of hers

7. The children's toys

8. Both twins' dinner

9. It's unfortunate but true

10. The young lass's smile

B. 1. It's true that when famous wit Dorothy Parker was told that President Coolidge, also known as "Silent Cal," was dead, she exclaimed, "How can they tell?"

2. When a woman seated next to Coolidge at a dinner party once told him she had made a bet with a friend that she could get more than two words out of him, he replied, "You lose."

3. Twenty-one of Elvis Presley's albums have sold over a million copies; twenty of The Beatles' albums have also done so.

4. Cinderella's stepmother wasn't pleased that her daughter received an "F" in her creative writing class on her poem "Seven Guys and a Gal," which she had plagiarized from her two friends Snow White and Dopey.

5. "Wasn't it Mae West who said, 'When choosing between two evils, I always like to try the one I've never tried before'?" asked Olivia.

6. Horace said, "Believe me, it's to everybody's advantage to sing the popular

song 'You Stole My Heart and Stomped That Sucker Flat,' if that's what the holdup man wants."

7. A scholar's research has revealed that the five most commonly used words in written English are "the," "of, "and," "a," and "to." (Underlining the words in quotation marks would also be correct.)

8. The triplets' mother said that while it's hard for her to choose, O. Henry's famous short story "The Ransom of Red Chief' is probably her favorite.

9. Despite both her lawyers' advice, she used the words "terrifying," "hideous," and "unforgettable" to describe her latest flight on Golden Fleece Airways, piloted by Jack "One-Eye" Marcus. (Underlining "terrifying," "hideous," and "unforgettable" would also be correct.)

10. It's clear that Bubba didn't know if the Christmas tree thrown in the neighbors' yard was ours, theirs, or yours.

Pratice, p. 483

1. Many moviegoers know that the ape in <u>King Kong</u> (the original 1933 version, not the remake) was only an eighteen-inch-tall animated figure, but not everyone realizes that the Red Sea Moses parted in the 1923 movie of <u>The Ten Commandments</u> was a quivering slab of Jell-O sliced down the middle.

2. We recall the last words of General John B. Sedwick at the Battle of Spotsylvania in 1864: "They couldn't hit an elephant at this dist . . .

3. In a person-to-person telephone call, the twenty-five-year-old starlet promised the hard-working gossip columnist that she would "tell the truth and nothing but the truth" about her highly publicized feud with her exhusband, editor-in-chief of <u>Meat-Eaters' Digest.</u>

4. While sailing across the Atlantic on board the celebrity-filled yacht the "Titanic II," Dottie Mae Haskell (she's the author of the popular new self-help book <u>Finding Wolves to Raise Your Children</u>) confided that until recently, she thought "chutzpah" was an Italian side dish. (Dashes instead of parentheses would be correct too.)

5. During their twenty-four-hour sit-in at the melt-down site, the anti-nuclear protesters began to sing, "Oh, say can you see. . . .

6. Few people know that James Arness (later Matt Dillon in the long-running television series <u>Gunsmoke</u>) got his start by playing the vegetable creature in the

postwar monster movie <u>The Thing</u> (1951). (For more emphasis, substitute dashes for the parentheses.)

7. Similarly, well-known T.V. star Michael Landon, who died of cancer in 1991, played the leading role in the 1957 classic <u>I Was a Teenage Werewolf.</u>

8. A French chemist named Georges Claude invented the first neon sign in 1910. (For additional information on his successful attempts to use seawater to generate electricity, see pp. 200–205.)

9. When Lucille Ball, star of <u>I Love Lucy,</u> became pregnant with her first child, the network executives decided that the word <u>expecting</u> could be used on the air to refer to her condition, but not the word <u>pregnant.</u> ("expecting" and "pregnant" are also correct.)

10. In mystery stories, the detective often advises the police to <u>cherchez la femme.</u> [Editor's note: Cherchez la femme means "look for the woman" in French.]

CHAPTER 19: A CONCISE GUIDE TO MECHANICS
P. 485

SUMMARY

CAPITALIZATION

ABBREVIATIONS

NUMBERS
Practice, p. 488

SPELLING

ANSWERS TO "PRACTICE" EXERCISES

Practice, p. 488

A. 1. delicious Chinese food

2. Memorial Day memories

3. fiery Southwestern salsa

4. his latest novel, *The Story of a Prince Among Thieves*

5. my son's wedding at the Baptist church

6. Count Dracula's castle in Transylvania

7. African-American heritage

8. a Dodge van driven across the Golden Gate Bridge

9. Sunday morning newspapers

10. the British daughter-in-law of Senator Snort

B. 1. Speaking to students at Galludet University, Marian Wright Edelman, founder and president of the Children's Defense Fund, noted that an American child is born into poverty every 30 seconds, is born to a teen mother every 60 seconds, is abused or neglected every 26 seconds, is arrested for a violent crime every 5 minutes, and is killed by a gun every 2 hours.

2. My sister, who lives in the East, was amazed to read studies by Thomas Radecki, M.D., showing that 12-year-olds commit 300% more murders than did the same age group thirty years ago.

3. In 67 A.D. the Roman Emperor Nero entered the chariot race at the Olympic Games, and although he failed to finish the race, the judges unanimously declared him the winner.

4. According to John Alcock, a behavioral ecologist at Arizona State University, in the U.S.A. the chances of being poisoned by a snake are 20 times less than those of being hit by lightning and 300 times less than the risk of being murdered by a fellow American.

5. The official Chinese News Agency, located in the city of Xinhua, estimates that there are ten million guitar players in their country today, an amazing number considering that the instrument had been banned during the Cultural Revolution that lasted ten years, from 1966 to 1976.

6. Two hundred thirty-one Electoral votes were cast for James Monroe but only one for John Quincy Adams in the 1820 presidential race.

7. The British soldier T. E. Lawrence, better known as "Lawrence of Arabia," stood less than five feet, six inches tall.

8. Drinking a glass of French wine makes me giddy before my ten o'clock English class, held in Wrigley Field every other Friday except on New Year's Day.

9. When a political opponent once called him "two-faced," President Lincoln retorted, "If I had another face, do you think I would wear this one?"

10. Alexander Graham Bell, inventor of the telephone, died in Nova Scotia on August 2, 1922; two days later, on the day of his burial, for one minute no telephone in North America was allowed to ring.

SECTION THREE

PART FIVE
ADDITIONAL READINGS

CHAPTER 20: EXPOSITION: DEVELOPMENT
BY EXAMPLE
P. 495

"DARKNESS AT NOON"—P. 495

Questions on Content, Structure, and Style

1. What is Krents's thesis: is it clearly stated?

2. How does Krents support his claims?

3. Of the examples presented, which is most effective? Why?

4. Which of Krents's examples is least effective? Explain.

5. Are there any points raised by Krents that would be strengthened by additional illustrative examples? Explain.

6. What is Krents's purpose in writing this essay? Who is his intended audience?

7. Describe Krents's tone (e.g., "at which point even my saint-like disposition deserted me").

8. What does Krents mean when he writes in his opening paragraph that he sees himself only in "the image I create in the eye of the observer. To date it has not been narcissistic"? Contrast this paragraph with his conclusion. Do they address the same issue? Why or why not?

9. How is Krents's essay organized? Does it follow a logical, effective order?

10. This essay was originally published in 1976. Is it still relevant today? Have Krents's hopes for the future come to pass? Cite examples to support your answer.

Answers to Questions

1. Krents's thesis is not overtly stated; instead, his claim that handicapped individuals are the victims of ignorance-based discrimination is implicit in the essay.

2. The author's claim is supported with several personal experiences.

3. Students might argue that the hospital example, because of its vivid detail and dialogue use, is the most effective.

4. The example of being "turned down by over forty law firms" is perhaps less effective than the others since it is presented in such general terms. Krents notes that this "will always remain one of the most disillusioning experiences" of his life, yet it is not described in detail.

5. Showing one of the law firm rejections in detail, using dialogue and the same level of specific sensory detail as he did in the hospital example, would make Krents's description of this experience more powerful for the reader.

6. Krents's purpose in writing this essay, originally published for a general audience in The New York Times, is to show nonhandicapped readers how ignorance and misperceptions can lead to discrimination.

7. Krents uses a combination of humorous examples—to illustrate the ludicrous treatment of the handicapped—and honest, straightforward statements of frustration and hope to drive his points home.

8. The opening paragraph indicates that as he is blind, Krents "sees" himself as others see him, and because of public misperceptions it is not an overly flattering image. His concluding paragraphs imply that these misperceptions do not have to exist. Just as the young girl, in the innocence of childhood, does not recognize the handicap, so too can the plant manager learn to look beyond physical disabilities.

9. Krents's essay is organized logically by example, moving from instances where he experiences discrimination to experiences illustrating his hope that this discrimination will end.

10. Student responses to this question will vary, but all should be supported by examples. With fully developed examples, answers to this question could serve as the basis for student essays.

Vocabulary
1. narcissistic (1)—characterized by excessive love of self

2. enunciating (2)—pronouncing

3. conversely (2)—reciprocally, contrarily

4. graphically (5)—powerfully

5. disposition (13)—temperament

6. cum laude (15)—with distinction

"Black Men in Public Spaces"—p. 497
Questions on Content, Structure, and Style

1. What effect on the reader does Stables intend with his opening line?

2. Does Staples use primarily hypothetical or specific examples as support? Why does he make that choice for this particular essay?

3. In paragraph 6 and 7, the author tells of his boyhood in Chester, Pa. Why does he include this information?

4. Is Staple's thesis statement implicit or explicit? Write a thesis statement for this essay in your own words.

5. Staples includes an example in paragraph 10 or another black male journalist who experienced a similar negative reaction. Why does Staples include this example in addition to his own?

6. What are some of the more vivid details the author used to develop his examples? What is the impact of those details on the reader?

7. This essay was written in 1986. Do you believe these same experiences could happen today? In your community?

8. What prejudices have you experienced or witnessed? Besides race, what other stereotypes are held today and are causing people to be pre-judged? Are stereotypes always negative?

9. In paragraph 5, Staples says "young black males are overrepresented among the perpetrators of that violence [toward women]." What does he mean? Why does he acknowledge that fact?

10. What is the tone of this essay? What evidence can you cite to support your answer? Does the conclusive paragraph provide evidence that Staples has adequately learned to deal with the problem, or is there evidence of some residual bitterness in the conclusion?

Answers to Questions

1. Staples intends to shock the reader to attention with this overstated, purposeful misrepresentation of his experience.

2. The specific, *real* examples are important in this essay because, without them, a reader might accuse Staples of whining or misinterpreting people's actions. When he provides exact incidences, the reader can see how often Staples actually was pre-judged and understand how frustrating those experiences must have been for him.

3. Knowing that Staples was a "good kid" and that, while he saw violence in his home town, he was not part of it, is important for the reader in order to understand why he was so surprised at the reactions he received. Also, he was "scarcely noticeable" in his hometown in contrast to the constant awareness and suspicion he experienced in Chicago and New York.

4. The complexity of Staples's thesis is not explicitly stated in the essay, although a very concise summary of the topic appears in paragraph 11: "Over the years, I learned to smother the rage I felt at so often being taken for a criminal." A more complete thesis statement would include a clearer indication of his attitude toward these experiences: "After many negative experiences of being stereotyped as a potential criminal, I have unfortunately had to change my appearance and behavior to avoid being perceived as threatening because of my race."

5. Showing that other black males have the same experiences indicates the problem is larger than just his own and that he has not imagined or exaggerated his situation.

6. Staples describes himself ("a broad six feet two inches with a beard and billowing hair, both hands shoved into the pockets of a bulky military jacket") so that the reader can imagine the vision that threatened his "victim." The "thunk, thunk, thunk" of the door locks is also easy to imagine. The jewelry store owner ("her eyes bulging nearly out of her head") and her "enormous red Doberman pinscher straining at the end of a leash" help the reader picture the fear people feel when he confronts them.

7. Student responses will vary.

8. Students can relate to Staples's experience more closely when they discuss the types of stereotyping in which they have been involved. Teenagers certainly are stereotyped and others have instant stock reactions to them in many cases. They might also discuss religious and gender prejudices they have experienced.

9. Students often misread this statement. They often think Staples is saying that blacks are incorrectly suspected of being violent while he is actually conceding that more blacks than whites *are*, in fact, perpetrators of violence against women—he's just not one of them. This concession is important to show the reader is attempting to be very fair about his observations.

10. Student opinions will differ vary strongly on this question. Some will believe Staples is comfortable with the adjustment he has made while others will see an underlying edge to his resignation with the system. Staples's tone is not lividly angry, but he is unhappy that his race has to live with and accommodate such prejudice.

Vocabulary
1. unwieldy (2)—hard to manage

2. dicey (2)—questionable

3. errant (2)—wandering from a regular course

4. taut (4)—tight, tense

5. warrenlike (5)—as a crowded group of buildings

6. solace (5)—consolation, comfort

7. perilous (8)—dangerous

8. ad hoc (8)—for this case only

9. skittish (11)—easily frightened

10. congenial (11)—friendly, compatible

"RAMBOS OF THE ROAD"—P. 500
Questions on Content, Structure, and Style
1. Where do you find Gottfried's thesis statement?

2. Why does Gottfried choose to begin with a description of the Rambodriver he encountered rather than a introductory paragraph and thesis statement?

3. Where has Gottfried used comparison/contrast to illustrate his point more clearly?

4. Why is it more effective for Gottfried to give more than the first example of his Rambo encounters?

5. What is the purpose of this essay beyond entertaining the reader with stories of traffic fiends?

6. What are some of the descriptive terms and phrases used in this essay that make the experiences easy for the reader to "see"?

7. Why does Gottfried mention his passengers' feelings and his fear when the truck crowded him off the road?

8. The author uses first person; "I" is used frequently throughout this essay. Is the use of first person here appropriate? Why or why not?

9. Gottfried's article was first published in 1986. Has aggressive driving increased or decreased since that time? What specific examples could you cite as evidence for your response?

10. Gottfried's examples are mini-narratives, stories about his meetings with uncivilized drivers. Why then do we classify this essay as developed by example rather than narrative?

Answers to Questions

1. The thesis statement is the first line of paragraph 5.

2. The startling, exaggerated description pulls the reader in immediately to Gottfried's experience and helps the reader live the experience with the writer. Gottfried has used his experience as his attention-getter.

3. In paragraph 7, Gottfried compares his recent observations to a more civilized time.

4. One example might be an isolated case, not the trend or change Gottfried is trying to establish.

5. Gottfried's purpose is to point out the current trend toward viciousness behind the wheel which he has experienced in several different settings.

6. A list of descriptive details might include the following: glared at us with sullen intensity, comparison to Robert DeNiro, small sleeping town, elbowing fenders, beetle-eyed drivers, squeezing the steering wheels, the "behemoth" of a truck, etc.

7. The feelings are as important as the actions in Gottfried's examples because he wants the reader to know the intent of the Rambos is to intimidate and scare their victims.

8. The use of first person is appropriate and effective here because these are all Gottfried's experiences and observations; to use another voice might be artificial and distant.

9. Student responses will vary. This question provides the opportunity for students to practice summary/response on a small scale and would be a good first assignment when studying Chapter 16, Special Assignments.

10. If the essay stopped after paragraph 4, it would be a narrative from which readers could draw some conclusions on their own. As the essay stands, it has several examples from different times and places which illustrate a point the author explains clearly. (Careful attention to this question may help students make this distinction, a distinction which seems to be a problem for less sophisticated writers.)

Vocabulary
  1. sullen (1)—showing resentment by gloomy or ill-tempered behavior; withdrawn

  2. affront (2)—an open or intentional insult

  3. indignation (2)—anger mixed with disgust

  4. lunacy (3)—craziness

  5. behemoth (5)—a huge animal

  6. coupe (5)—a closed, two-door automobile

  7. testy (7)—easily irritated

CHAPTER 21: EXPOSITION: PROCESS ANALYSIS
P. 503

"ATTITUDE"—P. 503

Questions on Content, Structure, and Style

1. Is Keillor's "Attitude" a true process analysis essay? If so, what type is it—directional or informative?

2. What is Keillor's thesis? Is it stated or implied?

3. Is Keillor's introduction overlong? Why or why not?

4. Keillor writes, "For the first time in my life . . . I find myself taking the game seriously." Does he? Explain.

5. Is the "attitude" problem Keillor describes confined to slow-pitch softball?

6. In Shakespeare's Hamlet, the prince tells his mother, the queen, "Assume a virtue if you have it not." Does this line parallel Keillor's thinking?

7. Where did Keillor come up with the actions for improving attitude he describes in his "list"? Did he simply make them up?

8. Evaluate the first two sentences in paragraph 2. Are these sentences grammatical? If not, are the errors intentional? Why?

9. Characterize the tone of Keillor's essay.

10. Is Keillor's conclusion effective? Why or why not?

Answers to Questions

1. "Attitude" is a humorous how-to essay. It is directional—though it's debatable if anyone would actually follow his instructions.

2. He claims that, regardless of ball-playing skills, one must have a winning attitude. The thesis is implied.

3. Though the introduction is long, it is necessarily so. He uses the space to establish his ideas. Too, by relating these anecdotes, his purpose in giving his how-to "list" of methods to improve your softball-playing attitude is made clearer.

4. The nature of the essay suggests that he does not take the game as seriously as he claims. Of course, he's a humorist, but some of what he says is indeed serious, 125

though not presented in a serious way. Attitude is important, though he exaggerates its worth in this instance.

5. Obviously, answers will vary, but one could argue that the "attitude" problem described applies to many aspects of our lives. Sometimes a winning "attitude" is more important than skill.

6. Yes—at least to some extent. Keillor, despite the humor with which he presents the idea and the limited scope he applies it to, makes a valid statement about character. Sometimes if one acts a certain way, that behavior can influence performance.

7. All the actions he describes are, in fact, common sights in major-league baseball.

8. The sentences are fragments, but they are "grammatical" ones, used effectively for both transition and emphasis.

9. The essay is obviously humorous, but how it's humorous is important. It seems to walk a fine line between satire and slapstick.

10. The single sentence ending effectively punctuates the entire essay. The essay ends rather like one of Keillor's monologues on his public radio series, *A Prairie Home Companion.*

Vocabulary
1. trigenarians (1)—people in their thirties

2. quadros (1)—people in their forties

"DITCH DIVING" — P. 506
Questions on Content, Structure, and Style
1. What is the purpose of this essay? What is the expected audience?

2. What are the three steps in the process of ditch diving?

3. Bodett's essay is a "take-off," a humorous creation fashioned after another usually more serious model. What is the "model" he uses for a pattern? What parts of the model does he copy?

4. Often a process analysis tells the reader not only what to do, but what not to do. When does Bodett use this technique?

5. Effective process analyses also include a description of any necessary materials and/or tools. Where does Bodett use this technique?

6. Clever and unusual word choice is a frequent feature of humor. What word choices contribute to Bodett's humorous tone?

7. How does Bodett say one can distinguish a poor ditch diver from a better one?

8. Where does the author use examples to illustrate the steps?

9. Where and how does Bodett summarize the process?

10. What activities could you use to create a similar "take-off" What would the steps be?

Answers to Questions

1. The purpose is to entertain readers who have experienced difficult winters and have probably spent time trying to avoid disasters on wintry roads.

2. 1) leaving the roadway

   2) placing the vehicle

   3) asking for assistance

3. The essay models the real sport of diving. He describes the features which determine the quality of the ditch diving performance (elegance, artistry, competence) just as one might describe the features of a good dive into the pool (fluidity, height, cleanness). The "scoring" in points for creativity and degrees of difficulty allude to that same system in the judging of a swimmer's dive. The author continually tells how best to play to the judges.

4. In paragraph 1, Bodett lists the equipment needed: "a road, a ditch, some snow on the ground, and any licensed highway vehicle or its equivalent."

5. A ditch diver should never give a boring or even a simply honest reason for the accident (paragraph 4). Novice ditch divers should never attempt to position the car with wheels off the ground (paragraph 6). Those who want to score well should also never take the easy way of getting assistance such as merely walking to a phone (paragraph 7).

6. The mock serious tone and precision of many of Bodett's phrases is clever: "The manner and theme of your dive. . . ." "Nosed-in within ten degrees of level. . . ." "master class ditch divers" "exercising this art to excess." Bodett also uses exaggeration and hyperbole: "neatly enshrined" "undervalued creative medium." The final phrase, "dive carefully," is a fun and obvious play on words guaranteed to make the reader groan.

7. Superior ditch divers don't settle for the ordinary slide; they go to extremes with pizazz. Good ditch divers are artists. Their cars end up in precarious positions and they over-dramatize the cause of their slide. Bad ditch divers just have minor accidents.

8. In paragraph 4, Bodett uses hypothetical examples to suggest the types of reasons a driver might give for ending up in the ditch. In paragraph 6, he again uses examples to further develop the types of positioning a driver might do. Bodett uses the same technique with the hypothetical examples in paragraph 8 which illustrate the step of asking for help, and then for further support (paragraph 9), he uses a feigned specific example of his own winning plea for assistance.

9. In the concluding paragraph Bodett summarizes the process in a casual, dialogue-style language which is repetitive and rhythmic: "Hit 'er hard, sink 'er deep, get 'er out. . . ."

10. Students responses will vary.

Vocabulary
1. aesthetics (1)—artistry and beauty

2. panache (5)— flamboyance; dashing, carefree elegance

3. piker (7)—one who gambles in an overly cautious way

4. berm (8)—the raised bank along the side of a paved road

5. addle-brained (9)—muddled, confused

"THE JEANING OF AMERICA"—*P. 508*
Questions on Content, Structure, and Style
1. Quinn maintains that jeans are a symbol of the American way of life. What do they symbolize?

2. What are the main stages or steps in this process analysis?

3. This essay follows the development of blue jeans to 1978 when it was written. What stages would you add to the process to bring it up to date?

4. What does the narrative of Strauss's life add to this process analysis?

5. What descriptive details add more interest to the process of the invention and development of blue jeans?

6. Why do you think Quinn has chosen this topic to research and write about? What is her audience and purpose?

7. Where do you see transitional devises used to tie pieces of the process together?

8. What strategy does Quinn use to develop the concluding paragraph?

9. Our American culture has been known as a "melting pot" of many other cultures, and everywhere we can find French, English, Spanish, and German influences, among various others. What other distinctly American institutions/practices/objects such as blue jeans can you think of?

10. What objects which are an accepted part of your life might be interesting to trace back to their origins?

Answers to Questions

1. Blue jeans symbolize equality, ruggedness, frontier spirit and innovation.

2. a) Strauss goes west with canvas because he cannot make a living with his brothers.

   b) Strauss encounters a miner who complains about wearing out his pants.

   c) Strauss makes the miner pants from his fabric and the miner is enthusiastic about them.

   d) Fabric is changed to serge de Nimes (denim) by accident.

   e) Rivets are added by Davis as a joke.

   f) Easterners discover jeans in the 1950s at dude ranches.

   g) Popularity explodes during WWII with factory workers.

   h) Jeans are made all over the world and sold in great numbers.

3. Students might mention that there are now a multitude of manufacturers, styles, and colors; that the jean "look" has come to jackets, skirts, shirts, and shorts; that they are never supposed to look new now, but stone-washed and worn; that a whole new fashion statement has developed with torn, frayed, patched, and bleach-spotted jeans; or that "vintage jeans" have become an international phenomenon.

4. Without Strauss's personal history, the analysis would be a dry listing of events and dates; his story humanizes the process. Students might be encouraged to personalize their essays with anecdotes when appropriate.

5. Descriptive details that enliven the process are specific names, particularly Alkalai Ike, hauling 180 pounds of goods door to door, the fabric names and derivation of the term "jeans," numbers of jeans sold, and many others.

6. Quinn could be sure, when she picked this topic, that a broad readership would take blue jeans for granted and might be intrigued by the interesting and quirky process by which they were created and developed. Her purpose is probably both informative and entertaining.

7. Since the essay is arranged temporally, transitions related to time are used throughout: for two years, when, by this time, each year, etc.

8. The conclusion is a paragraph developed by example.

9. There are many possibilities for response such as barbecuing, rodeo, hot dogs, and football.

10. Students will find many objects they take for granted but seldom to they know how the object came to exist: skis, sunglasses, CDs, computers, neckties, Stetsons or ball caps, pieces of sports equipment (e.g., the refinement of baseball bats), etc.

Vocabulary

1. ubiquitous (2)—seeming to be present everywhere

2. emigrated (3)—departed from a place or country

3. eke (3)—manage to make a living (or find a solution) with difficulty

4. beckoned (4)—called or summoned by a slight gesture

5. pacify (5)—to calm, make peaceful

6. prospered (6)—thrived, flourished

7. commodity (6)—an article bought or sold

8. proletarian (6)—working class

9. idiosyncratic (6)—having a peculiar personal mannerism

Chapter 22: Exposition: Comparison/Contrast
p. 511

"Columbus and the Moon" —p. 511
Questions on Content, Structure, and Style

1. Beyond showing the similarities of the two explorations, what is Wolfe's purpose in this comparison/contrast essay?

2. What audience has Wolfe targeted? What evidence of content and word choice points to that target?

3. What method of organization has Wolfe chosen? Why?

4. What are the points of comparison Wolfe uses?

5. Point out some of the transitional devices Wolfe uses to switch from point to point and from subject to subject.

6. Is the essay primarily a comparison or a contrast of these two projects, or is it equally balanced between similarities and differences?

7. To what does the last line of paragraph 5 allude? What is the effect of Wolfe's allusion? The tone of the allusion?

8. Wolfe has a knack for addressing sophisticated topics in a very casual, reader-oriented and sometimes irreverent way. What diction (word choice) adds to this style?

9. Is there an argument in Wolfe's essay for or against NASA's exploration of space? Do you think Wolfe would be in favor of NASA's further exploration?

10. What other current events have some kind of parallel in history? What similarities and differences might help readers see the current situation in a larger context, or more realistically? What personal experiences of yours have a parallel in your family's history? What could a reader gain from the comparison/contrast of these two happenings?

Answers to Questions

1. Wolfe's purpose is to encourage readers to take a more realistic attitude toward exploration and see it in its proper context rather than the idealized versions they often get in brief history lessons and the media.

2. Wolfe targets a general audience who is intellectually curious but who is not very informed beyond basic common knowledge about either event. The details of political, technological, geographic, financial, and social history are presented for an uninformed reader. Also, the diction indicates he is speaking to a casual audience, not professional or academic readers: "bad-mouthing Columbus" "The public had become gloriously bored. . . ." ". . . the light-bill level" ". . . failed to bring home the gold."

3. Point-by-point organization is used throughout. Because Wolfe compares so many features (seven) and includes so many details for each, a reader might have to look back to be reminded of those details and how they compare to the new subject if the author had used the block method. Also, the unexpected closeness of the comparison is emphasized when the points are seen right next to each other.

4. Points of comparison/contrast and Wolfe's analysis of each point for the subjects:

   1) What caused the government to support the project (both projects were spurred by inter-national competition)

   2) What made the project possible (the occurrence of major inventions in each case)

   3) Number of voyages made (each made multiple trips)

   4) Attitude of the government toward continuing project (both governments started to question the actual return from the projects)

   5) Attitude of the citizens toward continuing project (in both cases, citizens became disenchanted with supporting the projects)

   6) How NASA and Columbus managed to overcome objections (both used public relations "spins" to convince the public and government of the value of the endeavor)

   7) How project was eventually viewed by history (Columbus was remembered as a valiant adventurer who helped civilization go forward; The verdict is still out on NASA)

5. Several transitional devices are highlighted below:

   Paragraph 1—caught up in a sea **race**. . . the **same way** that. . . space **race** (repetition)

   Paragraph 2—. . .**much in the same way** that the United States. . .

   Paragraph 2—**Likewise**, it was only. . . .

   Paragraph 3—**But** NASA and. . . .

Paragraph 4—**Likewise** by the early 1970's. . . .

Paragraph 5—**In 1493,** . . . (to move the reader back in time to Columbus)

Paragraph 6—**NASA suffered no such ignominy,** of course, but. . . .

Paragraphs 8 and 9— Columbus **died** in 1509, nearly. . . .

NASA still **lives,** albeit in reduced. . . . (to note the contrast)

6. Wolfe points out primarily similarities between the two until the conclusion where he makes the point that it will take much more time before history's judgment is in on the value of NASA's exploration.

7. The allusion is to the words of the first US astronaut to walk on the moon. Neil Armstrong, as he put his foot on the moon's surface, said, "That's one small step for man, one giant leap for mankind." The effect is to cause the reader to wonder how true those idealized words really are. His tone is mildly sarcastic.

8. Word choices: "bad-mouthing Columbus," ". . . what earthly good is it to anyone back home?" "the Government was becoming testy" ". . . the moon was in economic terms pretty much what it looked like from Earth, a gray rock." ". . .watching the caloric waves ripple." ". . . failed to bring home the gold."

9. Although implied rather than explicit, Wolfe seems to argue that NASA's ventures should eventually be received with the same kind of legendary awe as Columbus's. The sheer awe of discovery, over time, will survive the current demand for a practical side to space exploration.

10. Student responses will vary.

Vocabulary

1. appropriations (5)—money set aside for a project

2. caloric waves (6)—shimmering appearance of heat radiating from a surface

3. lurid (7)—shocking, startling

"MY REAL CAR"—P. 479
Questions on Content, Structure, and Style

1. In order to be worth a reader's time, a comparison/contrast essay must have a point—a reason for looking at similarities and differences. Why does White compare these two vehicles?

2. Why does White spend much more time describing her "real" car than the new one?

3. A good comparison/contrast discusses parallel points about "Subject A" and "Subject B." What are the points White examines relative to the two cars?

4. To what senses does White appeal in her description of the two vehicles?

5. Much of what White tells the reader about her "real" car involves inconvenience. Where do you see glimpses of her affection for the car, despite its problems?

6. After reading about the new car, what do you think Bailey White's attitude is toward it?

7. What encounters with cars like the "real" car have you had on the road? What new perspective on those encounters might this essay give you?

8. From the description of the old car, what do you assume about White's abilities and personality?

9. If you took White for a ride in your car, or your family car, what observations might she make about it?

10. What object have you replaced that had sentimental value? Why was the replacement either a satisfaction or a disappointment for you?

Answers to Questions
1. White believes there is a certain emotional and sentimental value in possessions that cannot be equaled or replaced by a newer substitute.

2. The value and long-term connection with which White regards the old car is more important to her than the rather emotionless and sterile quality of the new car.

3. White compares exterior appearance, starting procedure, interior and comfort, sound, and ride ("We floated down the road").

4. White appeals to four of the senses: sight, touch, hearing, smell.

5. As well as several other places, White's last paragraph shows her connection to the car which she still enjoys; paragraph 8, "a little smell of me," also demonstrates her bond with the car.

6. White appears to appreciate the convenience and comfort of the new car, but doesn't have the affection for it that she will always have for the other automobile which is full of memories.

7. Students' answers will vary; many may comment that they will now understand there may be an interesting and clever person behind the wheel and that their stereotypes may be far from reality.

8. Again, students will have different ideas.

9. Student responses will vary.

10. Student responses will vary.

Vocabulary
   1. odometer (5)—a mileage gauge

   2. ominous (9)—threatening, sinister, menacing

"LIFE IN A BUNDLE OF LETTERS"—P. 516
Questions on Content, Structure, and Style
   1. What two subjects are examined in this essay? Does Goodman primarily compare or contrast them?

   2. What is Goodman's thesis? Is it implicit or clearly stated?

   3. What points of comparison/contrast are used? Of these points, which are the best developed? least developed?

   4. Is more attention given to one subject than another? Is this type of balance important to the essay? Why?

   5. Describe an audience that would be receptive to Goodman's essay.

   6. What is Goodman's purpose in writing this essay? What emotional response does she want to evoke in her readers?

   7. Does Goodman use a block or point-by-point organization, or a mixture of the two structures?

   8. Goodman has written that she believes it's "important for all of us to make links between our personal lives and public issues." How does she accomplish this in "Life in a Bundle of Letters"?

   9. Goodman does not use examples to support her comparison/contrast claim. Would such examples help illustrate her thesis? Why or why not?

10. Reread Goodman's conclusion, noting that she ends with a question directed to the reader. What effect does this have on her audience? Is this an effective concluding strategy?

Answers to Questions

1. Goodman contrasts letter writing and long distance calling.

2. Goodman's implicit thesis is that while long distance offers "immediate gratification" and convenience, the loss of letterwriting signals the end of a somehow gentler, more humane way of communication that lets us "say exactly what we mean" and later can provide us with a link to our past.

3. Points of contrast include speed, ease, cost, "talking" versus "telling," immediacy, and tangibility. Goodman's discussion of the convenience and immediacy of long distance versus the more leisurely pace of letters is well developed. Perhaps the most fully developed point is referred to in the opening and closing paragraphs—the ability of letters to connect us to our past. Less developed points include the cost difference—while it is touched on, Goodman does not emphasize this issue.

4. There is a fairly even blend of discussion of both long distance and letters. This balance allows the reader to examine both subjects fully and equally.

5. An audience of Goodman's contemporaries (others who have lived through the generational shift from letters to long distance) will empathize; younger readers of the long distance generation will consider an issue that may be new and thought provoking to them.

6. Goodman's purpose, is, in a broad sense, to entertain. She indirectly invites her readers to consider their own experiences and ask what they may have lost now that long distance has replaced letterwriting. The essay may evoke a poignant sense of loss in the reader.

7. Goodman's essay is roughly based on a point-by-point structure where her two subjects are presented side by side. Students might compare this essay to "Two Ways of Viewing the River" or "Grant and Lee: A Study in Contrasts" to clarify structural differences.

8. The advent of long distance is a public issue that has affected all of us in private ways as communication is among the most personal of issues. Goodman's use of her own experience forges the link between the public and the personal for the reader.

9. Detailed examples (e.g., a direct contrast of news she received by phone compared to news received by letter) might work well in the essay.

10. The reader's answer to Goodman's closing rhetorical question is, of course, that you cannot "wrap a lifetime of phone calls in a rubberband" for later perusal, so she leaves her audience in agreement with her essay, a powerful concluding strategy.

Vocabulary
 1. omen (5)—warning, sign

 2. intercontinental (5)—carried on between continents

 3. formulate (8)—devise, create, concoct

 4. nuances (9)—variations, shades, innuendos

 5. simultaneous (12)—concurrent, in unison, occurring at the same time

 6. ephemeral (13)—short-lived, transient, momentary

CHAPTER 23: EXPOSITION: DEFINITION
P. 519

"THE HEROES AMONG US" — P. 519

Questions on Content, Structure, and Style

1. What is Wolf's thesis?

2. Why is it important for Wolf to use the strategy of definition in this essay?

3. What term(s) is he defining?

4. This text suggests caution when using a dictionary definition in an essay. Is this dictionary quotation appropriate? Is it integrated well?

5. What claim does Wolf make regarding the confusion of the terms "hero" and "celebrity" by children?

6. What solution does Wolf offer for this confusion?

7. How effectively does Wolf develop his solution?

8. Where does the author give examples of the kinds of people he believes are heroes?

9. Make a list of people you and your peers would call heroes. Do their actions and motivations put them into the category of celebrity or hero according to Wolf's distinctions?

10. Read the short story by Stephen Crane on p. 614 of this text, "The Mystery of Heroism." Is Collins a hero according to Wolf's vision?

Answers to Questions

1. Wolf's thesis could be stated as follows: We often confuse heroism with celebrity, identifying famous people as heroes rather than those close to us who are more heroic.

2. Wolf argues, ultimately, that we should hold up everyday upstanding citizens to children as heroes and role models rather than celebrities. In order to make this claim clearly, he must first distinguish the two terms. Paragraph 2 is devoted to this task.

3. Wolf agrees with the dictionary that heroes exhibit "courageous acts or nobility of purpose."

139

4. Although citing "Webster" is off-putting to most educated audiences, Wolf integrates the definition in a sentence rather than just saying, "According to Webster, heroism is. . . ." And, although the definition is somewhat over-simplified as most dictionary definitions are when only one part is excerpted like this, for Wolf's purpose in this essay, it works.

5. Wolf believes television and movies influence children by blurring the distinction between heroes and celebrities. The media "offers children a world of shallow values."

6. Wolf thinks we should encourage children to admire "people who struggle to make their neighborhoods better places to live," people who "lift society and do not lean upon it."

7. Wolf's solution is not very effective because his charge that "we should encourage. . ." doesn't identify who "we" are, how children can be encouraged, how to negate the media's powerful influence, etc. Instead, his statement is a rather weak repetition of a frequently heard refrain without much more to offer. Developing with specifics and detail would be much more effective.

8. In paragraph 5, Wolf mentions the types of people who should, by definition, be classified as heroes. He does not, however, offer any specific examples that would be more compelling to a reader.

9. Student responses will vary.

10. According to the dictionary, Collins might be considered a hero because of the "or" in the definition. Collin's actions can be considered courageous while his motives were certainly not noble. Is the dictionary definition satisfactory?

Vocabulary
1. obscures (3)—conceals from view

2. gratification (3)—satisfaction

3. celluloid (5)—film used in making movies

4. candidly (6)—openly, honestly

Excerpt from "Slouching Towards Bethlehem"—p. 521

[Users of previous editions will recognize this excerpt which was previously titled "The Santa Ana." Ms. Didion requests the excerpt be titled as above.]

Questions on Content, Structure, and Style

1. Is Didion's clearly a definition essay? Why or why not?

2. Is Didion's definition of the Santa Ana objective or subjective?

3. What method does Didion use to begin her essay? Is her introduction effective?

4. What expository tactic or method does Didion use to explain the Santa Ana in paragraphs I and 2?

5. What expository tactics does Didion use in paragraph 3?

6. What kind of wind is the Santa Ana? What are the characteristics of this type of wind?

7. Characterize Didion's tone, or "voice," in this essay.

8. According to Didion, people mistakenly claim Southern California has no "weather" at all, when in fact it has "infrequent but violent extremes." What are these extremes?

9. Paragraph 5 is nearly a list, an almost journalistic account, of what happened during the fourteen-day Santa Ana of 1957. What purpose does this paragraph serve? How does it relate stylistically to the rest of the essay?

10. Who is Raymond Chandler?

Answers to Questions

1. Though the essay does define, it is also part comparison/contrast essay, part causal analysis, and part personal experience.

2. In terms of content, the essay is objective, factual. However, some passages are almost impressionistic, almost poetic, and she clearly puts herself in the essay.

3. She begins with a personal account of anticipating the Santa Ana, using the present tense. The method is highly effective, because it places the reader in the text the way a dry, "dictionary" type beginning could not. She records her anticipation (and anxiety), and we as readers then anticipate her coming account.

4. She uses causal analysis.

5. She uses comparison/contrast, and, to some extent, causal analysis.

6. See paragraph 3. It is a *foehn*.

7. Didion is known for her personal experience essays. Even here, in an essay that is largely objective, her personality is evident.

8. See paragraph 4.

9. It illustrates the potential severity of the Santa Ana, its devastating effects. It also provides a contrast to some of the more fluid, poetic passages, and because it is so stark—a series of facts and figures—it underscores Didion's point in the previous paragraph.

10. Chandler (1888-1959) was a U.S. novelist and is famous for his detective stories (including *The Big Sleep* and *Farewell, My Lovely*), featuring private eye Phillip Marlowe.

Vocabulary
1. mechanistic (1)—mechanical

2. ominously (2)—menacingly

3. malevolent (3)—exhibiting ill will or malice

4. leeward (3)—located away from the wind

5. incendiary (4)—involving arson, producing fire

6. apocalypse (6)—the events leading to the end of the world, as in the Revelation to St. John

"WHAT IS POVERTY?"—*P. 523*
Questions on Content, Structure, and Style
1. Summarize, as concisely as possible, Parker's definition of poverty.

2. What techniques does the author use to develop her definition? Note those that are especially effective.

3. Note the structure of the essay, with many paragraphs beginning "Poverty is . . ." Why is this effective?

4. What is Parker's purpose? Describe her intended audience (referred to as "you" in the essay; see paragraph 12).

5. As the biographical sketch of Parker at the beginning of the essay notes, little is known about her, including whether she is, in fact, writing from personal experience or whether she is an observer, using first person point of view for effect.

Does her identity matter to you as a reader, affecting the impact of the essay? Explain.

6. Is Parker aware of people who would be unsympathetic to her claims? If so, how does she address these people and their beliefs in the essay?

7. What parts of Parker's definition would be strengthened by additional development? Explain.

8. Parker relies on personal (subjective) experience to present her definition. Is this sufficient to convince her readers? Explain.

9. Characterize Parker's tone. She asks the reader to "listen without pity," yet does her tone evoke pity, or is it her subject that raises pity in the audience?

10. Compare Parker's opening and closing paragraphs. What emotional effect does she hope to have on her audience?

Answers to Questions

1. Parker defines poverty by powerfully describing how the poor must live—an existence of deprivation, illness, filth, fear, shame, and despair.

2. Parker employs a wrenching first-person narrative style that refers directly to the reader ("you") to describe and define poverty. She offers extensive, blunt personal illustrations of the daily life of the desperately poor, a stark contrast to the lives of most of her readers.

3. This repeated phrase jolts the reader with its relentlessness: over and over the phrase introduces a new horror to the reader, just as the poor must face ceaseless devastation.

4. Parker's purpose is to graphically reveal the true nature of poverty rather than offer a sanitized sociological definition. Her intended audience are those who have never known poverty and perhaps blame the poor for their condition.

5. Student responses to this question will vary; positions should be well explained.

6. Parker directly addresses individuals who are unsympathetic to the poor. Examples include paragraph 4 where she responds to the statement "Anybody can be clean." In paragraph 11 she notes, "But you say to me, there are schools." In both cases Parker answers the beliefs of these critics with her own experience.

7. Among the points that students might indicate need further development are those raised in paragraph 10 (children isolated from their peers by poverty; how

poverty tempts children toward crime, drugs, and alcohol). Additional development might underscore the cyclical nature of poverty that Parker implies.

8. Parker does not pretend to offer anything more than her own experience to her readers so this narrative emerges as a powerful personal statement. While the addition of outside evidence would broaden Parker's base of support, it might also diminish the raw strength of the essay.

9. While readers may find that they do feel pity for the situation Parker describes, the description itself is not maudlin or filled with pathos. Instead it is brutally direct and unflinching.

10. The opening and closing paragraphs of the essay highlight Parker's desire to move her reader to anger and action rather than passive sympathy.

Vocabulary
   1. privy (2)—latrine, outhouse

   2. chronic (3)—of a long duration or frequent recurrence

   3. oleo (4)—margarine

   4. pink eye (11)—highly contagious eye infection

Chapter 24: Exposition: Division/Classification
p. 527

"A Brush with Reality: Surprises in the Tube" — P. 527

Questions on Content, Structure, and Style

1. In Chapter 5, the definition and purpose of division are given: breaking apart a subject to help a reader understand it more easily. What does Bodanis want the reader to understand?

2. Does Bodanis account for all the parts of his subject in his division? Why is it important for him to include all components in detail?

3. How does Bodanis arrange the parts of his division? Why does he make this choice?

4. Who is Bodanis's audience? What word choices lead you to your conclusion?

5. Why are the details of the origin and nature of chalk included (paragraph 3)?

6. In describing each part, Bodanis usually explains its use in other products. Why does the author make those comparisons?

7. Why is the growing list of ingredients repeated at several points (paragraph 9, 12, and 13)?

8. Why doesn't the author explain the nature of formaldehyde (paragraph 12) as fully as other ingredients? Should he?

9. What is the tone of the essay? Is Bodanis making a claim about the value of toothpaste and/or similar household concoctions? Does he make any explicit judgments about such products?

10. What other products would a consumer be interested in understanding more completely by such an analysis? Hair spray? Deodorant? Ice cream (which Bodanis says, in another part of his book, has "leftover cattle parts that no one else wants")? Lunch meat? What product information do you know that would be beneficial to others?

Answers to Questions

1. The purpose of the division is much greater than just to list the ingredients of toothpaste. Bodanis wants the reader to be aware that many common products have questionable ingredients that we should not take so lightly.

2. Bodanis is very thorough and detailed in his analysis because he wants the reader to realize the extraordinary number and nature of ingredients in this substance we use without a care.

3. The parts are arranged according to two principles. Bodanis starts with the largest component and progresses to those used in smaller amounts. He also arranges from least offensive and potentially dangerous to the most hazardous ingredients.

4. The author is speaking to an average consumer, not a professional or academic audience which is evident in the way he describes the ingredients in very ordinary terms. Also, the tongue-in-cheek language choices reveal the fun he is having with his topic: "a large helping of gummy molecules," "seaweed ooze," "big gobs," "a host of other goodies," "an inviting mess," "camouflage operation." Bodanis also uses sarcasm: "Only two major chemicals are left to make the refreshing, cleansing substance we know as toothpaste (paragraph 9)."

5. The level of detail emphasizes the bizarre quality of this ingredient. "Chalk" would seem a little disagreeable to a reader. But Bodanis wants the reader to know the ingredient is far stranger; it is the "wickedly sharp outer skeleton that these creatures had to wrap around themselves to keep from getting chomped by all the slightly larger other ocean creatures." It is the content of "massed graves" with which we are scrubbing our teeth.

6. Showing the reader that these ingredients are used in other materials we would never consider ingesting leaves the question of why the ingredients should be acceptable in toothpaste.

7. Repeating the list emphasizes the absurdity and number of objectionable ingredients in this apparently beneficial substance.

8. While a reader might not recognize titanium dioxide or know its effects, formaldehyde is well known to anyone who has made it beyond biology class. The stark identification— just using the name and letting the reader's imagine do the rest— is more powerful than an explanation.

9. While Bodanis makes no explicit judgments about such products, the language suggests he believes products like this are massive overkill. For example, he suggests that the ingredient used to clean the surface of the teeth is actually doing major damage: "A certain amount of unduly enlarged extra-abrasive chalk fragments tear such cavernous pits into the teeth that future decay bacteria will be able to bunker down there and thrive. . ." Also, his conclusion, which says plain water works about as well as toothpaste, suggests he doesn't value the product highly.

10. Student responses will vary.

Vocabulary
1. splayed (1)—enlarged, expanded

2. abrading (4)—rubbing off by friction

3. carnage (5)—destruction and death

4. cavernous (5)—deep and hollow

5. bunker (5) to hide under protection

6. errant (5)—wandering from a regular course

7. gustatory (11)—taste

8. tout (11)—to praise highly

"PARTY MANNERS"—P. 530
Questions on Content, Structure, and Style
1. What is Grossman's thesis in this essay?

2. What reaction do you think Grossman wants from his readers?

3. Are Grossman's categories distinct or are they overlapping and ambiguous?

4. Is there a natural order to these categories? Why might the author have picked this order of presentation?

5. As you read, you probably thought of people you know and specific experiences you have had. What could Grossman have done to make his categories even more easy to picture?

6. The author is a medical professional. Does it surprise you that the director of a New York medical center would write like this? Grossman's tone and style in this essay are undoubtedly different from the writing voice he would use for an article for a medical journal. What does this tell you about his writing ability?

7. What does Grossman think of the typical party? What kind of a party do you suppose Grossman would really like?

8. Grossman says this party behavior results, in large part, from nervousness and being ill at ease in a social context. What do you do when you are socially uncomfortable?

9. What acquaintances do you have which fit into some of these categories?

10. What is a character type that Grossman left out, but you see frequently at parties?

Answers to Questions

1. Many people use a party as a medium for acting out their deficiencies or unresolved problems.

2. Students will have different ideas. Grossman probably wants readers to identify with their party experiences and see these types as legitimate, but he may also want readers to reflect on their own behavior and try to enjoy the "warmth and closeness of other human beings" (paragraph 9) instead of acting out.

3. Yes, the categories are quite distinct.

4. No strong natural order is evident, but Grossman may have picked the more neurotic types for the end in order to build up more clearly to his conclusion.

5. Students will give examples from their own experience; examples would enliven and validate Grossman's categories.

6. Competent writers are flexible; they can adjust their style, language, and tone to the purpose and audience they are addressing.

7. The author thinks the typical party is a psychologist's dream. He feels that party behavior is fake and neurotic. He might enjoy a party comprised of good friends who could be totally natural with each other or a party organized around a topic or cause which would keep people from their "pathologic" behavior.

8. Students will give examples from their own experience.

9. Students will give examples from their own experience.

10. Suggestions will vary.

Vocabulary

1. promenades (1)—public places for walking

2. ubiquitous (2)—seeming to be present everywhere

3. foibles (3)—small moral weaknesses

4. martyred (6)—having chosen to suffer

5. rueful (6)—causing sorrow or pity

6. haranguing (7)—giving a long, blustering, and pompous speech

7. cryptic (8)—having a hidden meaning

"COLLEGE PRESSURES"—*P. 532*
Questions on Content, Structure, and Style
  1. Is Zinsser's introduction too long? Is the length justifiable?

  2. Is Zinsser's use of the first person (the "I") appropriate? Why or why not?

  3. What general classes of college pressures does Zinsser cite?

  4. Are the transitions at paragraphs 22 and 31 effective?

  5. Evaluate Zinsser's language. Is the vocabulary level appropriate?

  6. Characterize the tone of the essay. Is it formal? informal?

  7. Is Zinsser's use of dialogue and anecdotes to illustrate his points effective?

  8. Which of the four pressures Zinsser discusses could students most easily relieve? How?

  9. Zinsser cites four main pressures, but discusses a fifth in some detail. What is it?

 10. Does Zinsser's conclusion detract from the impact of his essay? That is, when he begins to show how many other interests students have, how they may not be as "obsessed" as he has portrayed them, does that lessen the meaning of his message?

Answers to Questions
  1. The introduction *is* long—some 14 paragraphs. However, given the nature of the essay, and its tone and overall length, the long introduction seems entirely appropriate.

  2. Although the first person can sometimes be a shortcoming in certain types of essays, making the thesis seem merely subjective, here it works well. Zinsser is an authority on his subject. Too, his audience—presumably his academic colleagues—would likely find his firsthand knowledge and "voice" appealing, if not necessary.

  3. Economic, parental, peer, and self-induced.

4. The transition at paragraph 22 seems rather stilted, rather contrived. Consequently, the transition at paragraph 31, which is parallel to the one at paragraph 22, also seems rough.

5. Although Zinsser does not use particularly esoteric language or inflated diction, the reader needs to be well educated, or at least well read, to easily comprehend the author's meaning. The vocabulary level is rather high, but given the probable audience, fitting.

6. Despite some of the language used in the essay, the tone is quite informal, almost conversational.

7. In short, yes. A good "rule of thumb" for writers is to offer at least one concrete example for every abstraction. Zinsser's "stories," as he points out, are almost funny, but not entirely because they illustrate the symptoms of a serious problem. However, the anecdotes, and the dialogue, tend to make what could have been a dry, formal, abstract essay both engaging and penetrating.

8. Obviously, the self-inflicted pressure. However, one could argue, as Zinsser does, that "it will be the students' own business to break the circles in which they are trapped"—including pressures placed on them by economics, parents, and peers.

9. Though Zinsser does not specifically include it in his four pressures, a fifth would be the pressures placed on students by professors.

10. On the contrary, the conclusion seems to effectively underscore his point. The last few paragraphs—though they to some extent are simple qualifiers—suggest that the problem, though real, can be remedied.

Vocabulary

1. supplicants (9)—those who ask humbly or earnestly, as in prayer

2. balm (9)—something that soothes or comforts

3. matriculates (17)—enrolls

4. tenacity (23)—persistence, stubbornness

5. pauperism (38)—poverty, beggary

6. blithe (46)—cheerful, carefree

7. codified (47)—arranged systematically, as laws

8. circuitous (48)—roundabout

CHAPTER 25: EXPOSITION: CAUSAL ANALYSIS
P. 541

"KIDS IN THE MALL"—P. 541

Questions on Content, Structure, and Style

1. Does Kowinski emphasize causes, effects, or a chain reaction of causes and effects?

2. What question is this causal analysis designed to answer?

3. What causes of the development of mall culture does Kowinski identify?

4. What effects has the mall had on teenagers? What effects have teenagers had on the mall?

5. What family function does Kowinski say the mall serves?

6. What are some of the most effective specific examples illustrating the effects of malls?

7. Teens are learning work habits at the mall, but how does Kowinski say their lessons about working are different than in other environments?

8. Paragraphs 14 and 15 seem to make an abrupt change. Has Kowinski lost his focus, changed his opinion, or is the section a functional part of the essay as a whole?

9. Arguments develop frequently over whether television causes problems in society or whether it just reflects them—the standard chicken-or-the-egg question. How would Kowinski answer that question as it pertains to malls?

10. What other objects, institutions, or changes (such as the proliferation of cars) have had an important impact on teenagers' lives? What were the effects? What evidence could you give to link the two and convince a reader that one did cause the other?

Answers to Questions

1. Kowinski mentions the causes extremely briefly, but he is more concerned in this piece about the effects (see answers #4 and 5 below).

2. At the end of paragraph 2, Kowinski brings up the question he will seek to answer in his causal analysis: "But are these kids being harmed by the mall"—are the effects of the mall harmful?

3. Kowinski mentions the causes of the development of mall culture in paragraph 2:

   1) primarily the choice of the teens themselves

   2) two paycheck families

   3) single parent families

   4) parental encouragement; mall looked upon as a safe, supervised environment

   5) lack of alternative/boredom.

4. The author cites a few positive effects of the mall but concentrates on the negative effects of the mall's instilling consumer values in the teens.

   Negative effects

   1) goal in life is money and buying things

   2) pressure to wear the right clothes

   3) adult experiences too quickly; "hurried child" syndrome

   4) passivity rather than pro-activity

   5) only mindless jobs available, no critical thinking skills

   Positive effects

   1) structure provided which is lacking in home environment

   2) microcosm of the world to learn from

   3) teaches children how to survive in what will be our future world

5. Kowinski says the mall becomes a "structural mother" (paragraph 11) by encouraging their growth and the development of their values, and by providing them a safe resting place from the stresses of growing up.

6. The example in the introduction immediately pulls the reader in to the topic and shows the strength of the attachment teenagers have to a mall. In paragraph 10, Kowinski uses examples to illustrate the different ways in which a mall seems to provide a "home" atmosphere for teens. The most vivid example is the story he uses to illustrate the mindlessness of jobs in the mall, a girl whose goal is "to perfect the curl on top of the ice-cream cones" (paragraph 12). Also, Kowinski uses a specific example in his conclusion to let a teen speak for the essential nature of the mall in her life.

7. From these jobs which are very limited in scope, teenagers do learn "how to hold a job and take responsibility " (paragraph 12), but they have no chance of advancing from these menial positions and they are not learning any meaningful skills, information, or thinking patterns.

8. In these paragraphs, the author is admitting that there are some apparently visible positive effects and that, sadly enough, this positive impact may be preparing teens for a materialistic, consumer world that they will have to live in.

9. In paragraph 14, Kowinski argues that the mall reflects the values of society. "Attitudes about curiosity, initiative, self-expression, empathy, and disinterested learning aren't necessarily made in the mall; they are mirrored there. . . ."

10. Student responses will vary.

Vocabulary
 1. subtleties (3)—fine distinctions

 2. resonances (3)— reinforced, repeated conditions

 3. inestimable (7)—unable to be measured

 4. mores (8)—folkways that contribute to the welfare of society

 5. ramifications (8)—consequences

 6. plethora (8)—excess, overabundance

 7. unsavory (9)—unpleasant

 8. surrogate (9)—substitute

 9. denizens (10)—dwellers

10. infiltrate (12)—to pass through

11. empathy (14)—emotional identification with another

12. impertinence (16)—a thing of little value

"The Best Years of My Life"—p. 545
Questions on Content, Structure, and Style
 1. What pattern of organization does Rollins use for this essay: a causal chain, focusing on causes or effects, or both?

 2. What are the major effects of Rollins having had cancer?

 3. Why do you think Rollins is writing this essay and to whom do you suppose she intends to speak? Do you think you are part of Rollins's intended audience?

4. Even though you may not have had a life-threatening disease, what can this essay say to you?

5. Without glancing back at the essay, what effect of Rollins's cancer was most memorable? Why do you think that point stayed with you?

6. Where does Rollins incorporate examples in the development of her paragraphs? Explain, by selecting one of these paragraphs, the difference between showing and telling when developing a point.

7. Many good conclusions "come full circle" from the introduction; in other words, they complete a thought opened up in the introduction. Where does Rollins set up this type of conclusion in the early paragraphs of the essay?

8. Rollins spends little time discussing her cancer (cause) but concentrates on its effects. Why does that work in this essay?

9. Some writers might have approached this subject in a more sentimental and emotionally draining way. What are some of the phrases and statements that Rollins makes that set a much more light, almost humorous tone? Why do you think she wanted to create this tone?

10. Rollins says "A big part of happiness is noticing it." How can you relate this statement to your life?

Answers to Questions
1. For the main part of the essay, Rollins concentrates on effects. However, in paragraph 3, she uses a causal chain strategy to explain how people usually react to a traumatic event threatening their lives.

2. 1) Loss of fear, 2) hypochondria, 3) finding pleasure everywhere—hedonism, 4) freedom from guilt, 5) improved "taste" in men, 6) noticing happiness.

3. There are probably several reasons for writing this essay. Students may come up with a variety of purposes, but among them are to help cancer survivors cope in a more healthy fashion, and to share her discovery that living more positively is possible for anyone. Anyone can be part of Rollins's audience once they acknowledge the second, broader purpose.

4. Student answers will vary with their experience. Students can be encouraged, in responding to this question, to practice application of causal analysis concepts to their own experiences.

5. Again, students will choose different passages as most memorable. The discussion can carefully be guided to an understanding that specifics—quotations, descriptive details or experiences—are what impress readers.

6. Most of Rollins's paragraphs are developed with a classic example strategy. She makes a statement about an effect and then illustrates it with specific experiences. Note, for example, how paragraph 5 discusses loss of fear. Paragraph 6 relates her experience of writing her book which she claims she would not have had the courage to do otherwise.

7. Rollins's discussion of paradox in paragraph 2 sets up the conclusion. The reader is ready to accept the paradox after the well-developed effect paragraphs; at the beginning, the idea of being glad about having cancer may be hard for the reader to process.

8. The author need not discuss cancer and the physical and emotional impact it can impart because that is a widely known and accepted circumstance. Other topics where the cause is more individual, technical, or subtle, however, may need more development devoted to cause.

9. Rollins lightens up her essay with references to Hallmark cards, celebrations, slang ("just in case I croaked"), and primarily by laughing at herself ("Goody, it's the flu!").

10. Student answers will vary and may, in fact, lead to interesting topics on which to write.

Vocabulary
1. intrinsically (1)—naturally, essentially

2. chemotherapy (2)—administration of usually large doses of sometimes very caustic chemicals to combat disease

3. harrowing (2)—distressing; making uncomfortable

4. hypochondriac (7)—one who is anxious about his or her health and/or imagined illness

5. gynecologist (8)—a doctor specializing in the treatment of women's medical problems

6. orthopedist (8)—a doctor specializing in the treatment of bones and joints

7. parsimonious (9)—stingy

8. hedonism (10)—pleasure seeking

9. masochism (1 1)—getting pleasure from being dominated, mistreated, or hurt

10. voracious (11)—greedy, usually in eating

"THE TEACHER WHO CHANGED MY LIFE"—P. 549
Questions on Content, Structure, and Style

1. What is Gage's stated purpose in writing this essay? Are there other purposes as well?

2. According to Gage, what was Miss Hurd's greatest gift to him? What cause-and-effect relationship does this essay explore?

3. Gage's essay covers many years-nearly his lifetime, in fact. Why is this broad span of time important to his message?

4. What key scene best captures the essence of Gage's regard for Miss Hurd and her effect on his life? Explain your choice.

5. Are there any details given that are not vital to the central idea of the essay? Explain your selections.

6. Often, a key component of causal analysis essays is description. Choose two examples of effective description and indicate two sections of the essay where the reader might want more descriptive detail.

7. There are two key uses of dialogue in this essay. Find these sections and explain why Gage may have chosen to emphasize these particular moments, rather than others, with dialogue.

8. Consider Gage's use of transitions between paragraphs, listing examples of smooth transitions and noting those that are more abrupt.

9. The success of an essay can be judged by its impact on its readers. What specific audience would benefit from Gage's piece? Why?

10. Gage uses several examples of Miss Hurd's behavior to illustrate her character. What traits emerge in the following paragraphs: 6, 8, 11, 15, 16, 17 and 18, 22? Why is this a more effective way of revealing her character to the reader than simply telling the audience what she was like?

Answers to Questions

1. Gage concludes his essay by stating that it is a tribute to Marjorie Hurd, but his larger purpose is to tell a broad audience how a teacher can make a dramatic difference in someone's life.

2. Her greatest gift to Gage was "direct[ing] [his] grief and pain into writing," giving him a new interest that was to change his life and goals. Miss Hurd (the cause) inspired him to hone his writing skills (effect) and steered him toward writing about his family (effect) which led to Gage's career as a writer and journalist (effect).

3. Gage's goal is to show how Miss Hurd changed his life and this can only be accomplished if readers are allowed to see her continuing influence on him as he matures personally and professionally.

4. There are a number of possible answers to this question but because of its detail and emotional impact, the most likely choice is the portion presented in paragraphs 8–2 where Gage discusses writing about leaving Greece. Readers are allowed to see through Gage's eyes how Miss Hurd's prompting had a powerful impact on him.

5. Here, too, answers will vary. Some students might feel that the details of family celebrations are irrelevant (the music, the food, the dancing) while others might argue that all of Gage's descriptions are appropriate to the focus of his essay. Debate on this subject will help students clarify their own views of the relationship between essay focus and development.

6. Student responses will vary.

7. Gage uses dialogue twice: when he first introduces Miss Hurd (this allows his readers to "hear" her just as he did, making her real to his audience) and when Miss Hurd calls after President Reagan's mention of Gage's mother (here she is seen as caring and warm, a contrast to her earlier words that round out his characterization of her).

8. There are any number of smooth, effective transitions that students might cite. Some more abrupt shifts include the transition between paragraphs 14 and 15 as well as 16 and 17, and 20 and 21.

9. No one answer to this question is "right." Students might argue that would-be teachers and writers would particularly benefit from reading the essay.

10. Paragraph 6 reveals her toughness, paragraph 8 her insight, paragraph 11 her pride and kindness; the fifteenth paragraph shows her devotion, paragraph 16 her persistence, paragraphs 17 and 18 her compassion and thoughtfulness,

paragraph 22 her deep regard for Gage. If Gage had told his readers she possessed these traits, rather than showing Miss Hurd in action, her portrait would not be as vivid.

Vocabulary

1. refugee (1)—displaced person

2. portly (2)—plump

3. layabouts (6)—lazy people

4. honed (7)—sharpened

5. Iron Curtain (9)—political and ideological barrier isolating an area

6. mortified (11)—humiliated

7. balky (16)—hesitant, uncooperative

8. serpentine (19)—snakelike

9. void (20)—emptiness

10. bounty (21)—abundance, plenty

11. testament (21)—tribute

12. catalyst (21)—agent causing an action

13. emphatically (21)—strongly, vehemently

14. eulogy (22)—formal statement of tribute to someone delivered after their death

CHAPTER 26: ARGUMENTATION
P. 555

"U.S. KIDS NEED MORE SCHOOL TIME"—P. 555 AND
"THE SCHOOL YEAR NEEDS TO BE BETTER, NOT LONGER"—P. 557

Questions on Content, Structure, and Style

1. Which introduction, Goodman's or McCarthy's, is most effective and why?

2. What is the principle on which Goodman bases her argument?

3. Both Goodman and McCarthy agree that money is a major problem in education, but how do they differ in their opinions of how those dollars should be spent?

4. Which author deals more convincingly with the arguments of the opposition?

5. How would McCarthy respond to Goodman's argument?

6. What are the authors' arguments regarding the effect of summer vacation on educational gain?

7. Note the way each author uses the idea of "custodial care" of students in paragraph 6 (McCarthy) and paragraph 10 (Goodman). How do they differ on this issue and how have they used the term differently?

8. Describe the distinct difference in tone of these two essays. What is the impact of tone on the reader?

9. Both Goodman and McCarthy tie their conclusions neatly to their introductions. How does each writer accomplish this?

10. Which argument was more convincing? What personal experiences have you had that influenced your opinion?

Answers to Questions

1. Students may say Goodman's introduction gives the reader a picture with which to identify; McCarthy's introduction, on the other hand, is intended to be controversial and somewhat adversarial.

2. Goodman's premise is that school calendars have been designed to meet societal and family needs; needs have changed and so should calendars. Schools should be both custodial and educational.

159

3. Goodman believes money should be spent to extend the number of school days while McCarthy believes finances should be dedicated to recruiting and keeping more teaching talent.

4. Goodman cites one authority, but mostly makes reasonable, logical claims as support. Goodman does, however, raise a question in paragraph 7, rather than answering the opposition sufficiently. McCarthy uses more quotations, source citations, and examples as support.

5. McCarthy would say that longer is not better, that good teaching and quality learning will not automatically improve with more school days.

6. Goodman claims that there are educational losses over the "empty time" of summer vacation. McCarthy argues that summer vacation time offers an opportunity for extended learning and experiential education.

7. Although Goodman believes that schools do have some legitimate custodial authority, McCarthy uses the negative connotation of the word "custody" to describe the idea of keeping students in school longer.

8. McCarthy's tone is more antagonistic than Goodman's. The attitude of McCarthy might alienate professionals, but then they are probably not his audience. Goodman's tone is more moderate and would offend few readers.

9. Goodman begins and ends with the image of students hanging out, with the implication that a longer school year would solve this problem. McCarthy teases the reader at the beginning with the idea that students know more than experts, then ends by reaffirming that his students' comments show a better understanding of how financially starved schools are and what the hunger is really for.

10. Student responses will vary.

Vocabulary

1. makeshift (Goodman, 2)—a thing that will make do as a substitute

2. sacrosanct (Goodman, 4)—very holy or sacred

3. crux (Goodman, 9)—critical point

4. vouchers (Goodman, 10)—a paper serving as evidence of payment

5. calibrated (Goodman, 1 1)—measured, gauged

6. fretting (McCarthy, 3)—worrying

7. dolts (McCarthy, 4)—stupid, slow-witted people

8. innovative (McCarthy, 7)—bringing in something as new

9. niggardly (McCarthy, I 1)—given grudgingly

10. largess (McCarthy, I 1)—generosity

"How About Low-Cost Drugs for Addicts?"—P. 559

Questions on Content, Structure, and Style
1. What is Nizer's claim?

2. What key points of support does he offer for his position?

3. Which points are most/least convincingly developed? Explain.

4. Describe Nizer's argumentative style/tone. How did it affect you as a reader?

5. In paragraphs 11–15 Nizer addresses two opposition points. How successful is his refutation of these claims?

6. Are there points in support of or in opposition to Nizer's claim other than those given? List some possibilities.

7. Is Nizer's essay logically structured? Briefly describe how it is organized.

8. Identify any logical fallacies in this essay.

9. Consider the structure of paragraph 6 as Nizer repeats the phrase "This is why . . . ." How does this repetition affect the reader?

10. This essay appeared in *The New York Times* in 1986. After several more years of "the war on drugs" is Nizer's argument more relevant or less relevant now? Explain your view.

Answers to Questions
1. Nizer's claim is found in paragraph 2 where he states, "The government should create clinics, manned by psychiatrists, that would provide drugs for nominal charges or even free to addicts under controlled regulations."

2. Nizer claims that his solution will reduce the cost of the national effort to stem drug use and trafficking, and greatly reduce drug-related crime.

3. The essay's most fully developed point of support is the discussion of drug-related crime reduction (paragraphs 5–10). Detailed specifics and convincing statistics are cited. In contrast, the cost issue is not as thoroughly explored and would benefit from additional specific detail.

4. Nizer's tone is urgent. He appeals directly to the reader's sense of frustration with a burgeoning problem that seems beyond control.

5. It might be argued that Nizer's refutation of the two opposition points is limited by its lack of specific detail. For example, he does not explain exactly how the program will treat the problem of addiction, nor does he thoroughly explain how the system can avoid being cheated.

6. Among the additional points opposing Nizer's claim are the possibility of corruption and the possible spread of addiction to new users tempted by low costs.

7. Nizer's essay is logically organized as he presents his thesis first, followed by his main supporting points, and then addresses his opposition before concluding his argument.

8. Nizer presents his case rationally on the whole but there are some logical fallacies that students might note, including begging the question when he states, "all objections become trivial when matched with the crisis itself": his readers may not agree that all objections are trivial. The reference to China (paragraph 16) is possibly a faulty comparison as details proving a parallel between the U.S. and China in this instance are not given.

9. This repetition emphatically drives home the effects of the "new domestic terror" on U.S. society, a strong point for Nizer to accent since he claims that his proposal will solve this problem.

10. Responses to this question will vary but should be well supported with evidence and analysis.

Vocabulary
1. discrepancies (2)—variances

2. caches (4)—hiding places, secure storage places

3. pittance (6)—a small amount

4. profound (7)—deep, far-reaching

5. exacted (8)—forcibly obtained

6. compulsion (9)—irresistible urge to commit an irrational act

7. sordid (9)—dirty, filthy

8. salutary (1 1)—promoting health

A SCIENTIST: 'I AM THE ENEMY' —P. 561
Questions on Content, Structure, and Style

1. Why does Kline begin with the first, provocative line?

2. What is the author's thesis regarding the use of laboratory animals?

3. What examples of medical advances from animal research does Kline offer as evidence to support this thesis?

4. Why does Kline refer to several major arguments frequently used against animal experimentation? What is the main reason he disagrees with ani-experimentation activists?

5. How does Kline refute the argument that computer simulation is a legitimate alternative to experimentation?

6. How does the author use emotional appeals? Are they effective?

7. What concessions does the author make to show he does understand that activists have sometimes had legitimate concerns?

8. Describe Kline's tone. How does he gain the confidence of a skeptical reader?

9. Kline claims that a "vocal but misdirected minority" has had too much influence on politicians and legislation. Do you agree with his assessment? What is the majority opinion? What current issues are often influenced by the strong voices of minorities? What historical issues have been subject to the strong influence of a minority? Is it good or bad that minorities can have such impact?

10. Is Kline's overall argument convincing? How could you make it moreso? How might you argue against the essay?

Answers to Questions

1. Kline's blunt statement identifying himself as the enemy and the explanation of why he devotes his professional life to research personalize the opposition. Animal rights activists might find a villainous, heartless opponent more to their liking because it is much easier to demonize a vicious enemy. Kline's opening takes the fire out of that type of illogical and personal attack, and he

turns the argument toward the reasonable purposes for using animals in the laboratory.

2. Kline believes animal research is essential to the continued development of new therapies and innovative surgeries. He criticizes both the public and his peers involved in medical research for not defending what he believes is a legitimate and ethical practice.

3. In paragraph 7, Kline explains that vaccines, antibiotics, drugs, and advanced surgical procedures have been developed with animal research. (Students should be asked if these are specific or hypothetical. How do they know? How could Kline make these examples far more convincing?)

4. When he acknowledges the major arguments of those opposed to animal research, he shows an understanding of their viewpoint. By doing so, he has the opportunity to explain why those viewpoints are not correct. His major point for his side of the argument is that human lives can be saved, and human pain and suffering can be diminished with the technology and other medical knowledge from continued experimentation on animals. He believes this probable outcome is a higher value than any suffering inflicted on the animals.

5. He explains that computer simulated models cannot be as productive in medical research as they are in other sciences because of the inexactness of medicine and the complexity of biological systems.

6. Kline uses emotional appeals effectively to encourage the reader to apply the same kine of sympathy they might have for research animals to human beings in tragic medical circumstances. At the beginning of the essay, he compels the reader to see him as a humane researcher motivated by his concern for "healthy, happy children." In paragraph three, he argues that those on his side of the argument might have allied the public more closely have they resorted to the same types of emotional appeals as animal activists by "waving equally sad posters of children dying of leukemia or cystic fibrosis." The next paragraph cites other examples of children in tragic accidents; using children rather than the elderly with Parkinson's, for example, is calculated to pull at the reader's emotions. As he concludes (paragraph 8), he once more reminds readers that his opinions come from his watching "many children die, and their parents grieve," and charges them to have as much compassion for dying humans as they would for a dog or cat.

7. In paragraph 5, Kline does agree that computer simulation has some value, principally to offer technological models. In his concluding paragraph, he admits that activists have improved conditions for experimental animals and that they have encouraged scientists to use suitable alternatives.

8. Throughout the essay, Kline's tone is reasonable and non-threatening. He shows respect for his opposition rather than attempting to ridicule them; he gives activists credit in his conclusion for bringing attention to the humane treatment of animals involved in research.

9. Student responses will vary.

10. Students might add more detailed evidence of the many treatments and therapies that have been developed by using animal research, and evidence to substantiate that animals are indeed treated humanely in laboratory experiments. Those arguing against the essay might be reminded to maintain the reasonableness of their arguments as has Kline rather than resorting to purely emotional arguments.

Vocabulary
1. vilified (1)—made evil or sinful

2. inhumane (1)—cruel, brutal

3. simulation (2)—imitation, false resemblance

4. apathetic (2)—unfeeling

5. unconscionably (3)—unreasonably

6. malevolent (4)—wishing evil to others

7. placate (6)—to quiet or soothe anger

CHAPTER 27: DESCRIPTION
P. 565

"ODE TO THANKSGIVING"—P. 565

Questions on Content, Structure, and Style

1. Is Arlen's title ironic? Why or why not?

2. Humorists often use exaggeration. Give examples of effective uses of exaggeration in Arlen's essay.

3. Evaluate Arlen's style, especially his diction. Does his essay contain too many difficult or obscure words? Explain.

4. What reasons does Arlen give for proclaiming Thanksgiving a "mockery of a holiday"?

5. Is Arlen's essay focused? Is it concise? Why or why not?

6. Characterize Arlen's tone, or "voice."

7. Arlen blames part of the problem with Thanksgiving on the time of year that it occurs. Explain his "theory" about the "nowhereness" of the Thanksgiving season.

8. At the end of paragraph 2, Arlen describes a televised football game. What is his purpose here? What is the effect of this episode?

9. What symbols of Thanksgiving does Arlen criticize?

10. Evaluate Arlen's conclusion. Is this an effective way of ending his essay?

Answers to Questions

1. An ode is typically a lyrical poem in an exalted style that usually praises rather than condemns its subject, so Arlen's title is ironic.

2. Virtually any paragraph will provide examples.

3. Students may contend that Arlen uses too many "big" words—not only because they are unfamiliar with some of them but also because they have probably had writing teachers who admonished them to write simply. It should be noted the word choice is dependent on purpose. Here, Arlen is writing an "ode," which by definition demands lofty language. Even though this is a parody, the language fits his purpose.

4. Again, any paragraph will provide ample illustration. His main argument is that there's nothing about Thanksgiving to be thankful for.

5. Arlen sticks to one subject, primarily, but the essay is arguably overlong. He could have made his point in considerably less space and offered fewer examples.

6. His tone is sarcastic. He uses exaggeration to stress his point, which is largely tongue-in-cheek.

7. According to Arlen, Thanksgiving is a "nowhere" season: fall is past its prime and winter is still to come during this time of limbo.

8. He is satirizing the ritual of watching football on TV at Thanksgiving, of course. He exaggerates the silliness of the game and the activity of watching it. The men watch the game; the women prepare the meal. Neither event, as Arlen portrays them, is enticing.

9. See the opening paragraph.

10. He returns to the subject of Christmas, which he has touched upon earlier. His attitude towards this holiday is the same as his attitude towards Thanksgiving. One almost anticipates a sequel, "Ode to Christmas." The final phrase, "unrealistic expectations," effectively sums up Arlen's view of both holidays.

Vocabulary
1. provenance (1)—place of origin

2. forgather (1)—gather

3. aberrant (1)—deviating from the norm, distorted

4. interregnum (2)—a pause in continuity

5. corollary (2)—a natural consequence, result

6. torpid (3)—sluggish; in a lethargic, inactive state

7. nadir (4)—the lowest point

8. primeval (4)—of the earliest ages

9. surreptitious (4)—done by stealth, secret

"HUSH TIMMY—THIS IS LIKE A CHURCH" — P. 568
Questions on Content, Structure, and Style
1. What is the dominant impression Anderson intends his reader to have of the memorial? What metaphor does Anderson use to convey this impression?

2. What language choices help develop this metaphor?

3. A secondary theme is intertwined in the description, most notably in paragraphs 2, 5, and 10. What is this theme and what does it add to the description?

4. What kinds of research has Anderson done to create this very comprehensive description?

5. What are the most memorable details about the memorial? What do they add to the description?

6. In paragraph 2, Anderson gives his first visual description of the wall: "two skinny black granite triangles wedged onto a mound of Washington sod." What is the tone of that description? Why does he use such language and what is its effect?

7. Where does Anderson use elements of comparison and contrast to develop his description?

8. To what widely known quotation does the last line in paragraph 7 refer? How does this allusion develop the overall impression? How does the line relate to the physical wall itself?

9. Anderson quotes people with different connections to the memorial. What are those relationships? What does each add to the reader's understanding?

10. What place have you seen that has made an indelible impression on you? What metaphor might you use to enrich your description? What sorts of words and images could you use to emphasize the parallel? Who could you interview to add depth and breadth to your personal perspective? What additional research would you need to do?

Answers to Questions

1. Anderson wants the reader to feel the memorial is a holy place at which the visitor has nearly a religious experience. Anderson uses a church as the unifying metaphor throughout.

2. Paragraph 1, "sanctum. . . spiritual place."

   Paragraph 6, "sublime and stirring."

   Paragraph 7, "hush, Timmy — This is like a church." (and, of course, the title)

   Paragraph 7, "processionals. . . ritual. . . liturgical . . . valley of the shadow of death."

Paragraph 8, "a holy place."

Paragraph 10, "faithful reflections."

3. Anderson also emphasizes the numerous unexpected contrasts and surprises connected to the wall. He sets up this motif in paragraph 2, "beautiful and terrible." and concludes this essay with a visitor's comment that "No one expected that [the eerie reflections of a plane reminiscent of Viet Nam war planes.]" The public's strong response was unexpected, Maya Lin's Asian connection is a strong irony, and the conflict over literal or symbolic representations continues the tension of this theme. This secondary impression creates a feeling of ironic mystery and specialness to the memorial and underscores that the memorial has created a life of its own: "You don't set out and build a national shrine. . .It becomes one."

4. Interviews, historical information, visitor data, and details from the panels themselves are part of Anderson's research.

5. The number of names (58,022) help the reader relate to the enormity of the tragedy memorialized. Also, the increasingly large number of visitors shows that the mystique and power of the wall is growing rather than diminishing over time.

6. Anderson's tone is strikingly business-like and purposely understates the impact of the memorial. His language emphasizes the simplicity of the concept and sets up a contrast to the complexity of its meaning and effect on the public.

7. In paragraph 3, the author compares the memorial to the other famous memorials to presidents in the capital. He also compares the two opposing views of what style the memorial should be. Later, in paragraph 7, he compares the wall to the Western Wall in Jerusalem, a Jewish religious shrine.

8. The line is taken from the Lord's Prayer. The allusion reminds the reader of the holiness of the church metaphor. After this line in the prayer comes "I shall fear no evil." The allusion enlarges the metaphoric meaning of the wall, a sanctuary, where visitors are protected, sheltered, and dramatically affected in the "valley" in the ground where the memorial is located.

9. The wall's and statue's creators help clarify the purpose, history and design of the memorial. The park ranger's words set the wall apart from other Washington memorials in its surprising impact; her comments come from much experience watching visitors at all the major monuments, so they have the ring of authority. The veterans' comments are poignant, relating the reader emotionally to the "wall experience," and validating the effectiveness and appropriateness of the memorial.

10. Students responses will vary.

Vocabulary
1. redemptive (3)—serving to pay off or ransom

2. apolitical (4)—not relating to a particular political theory

3. elitist (5)—one who believes he is better than others by being part of a select or special group

4. stigmatized (5)—to mark or "brand" something as if it were disgraceful or not normal

5. sublime (6)—high in place; inspiring awe

6. figurative (6)—representative by likeness; typical

7. mandarins (6)—high, powerful officials

8. spectral (6)—resembling a ghost or spirit

9. wary (6)—cautious, suspicious

10. erstwhile (7)—at one time; former

11. liturgical (7)—having to do with prayer or worship

12. touchstone (7)—a test for genuineness

13. catharsis (7)—a purifying change

14. amphitheatrical (7)—like a valley or level place surrounded by rising ground similar to an ancient theater with seats rising up the circular sides

15. totem (8)—an animal or object taken to be a symbol of a clan

"THE MAN IN THE WATER"—P. 570

Questions on Content, Structure, and Style
1. What is Rosenblatt's thesis? Is it stated or implied?

2. What distinguishes this essay from merely factual accounts of similar events?

3. Paragraph 2 seems to be a pivotal paragraph. Why?.

4. Rosenblatt presents factual information about the other three heroes—their

names, their reasons for acting as they did. What effect does this have on his comments about the man in the water?

5. What is the "abiding wonder of the story" according to Rosenblatt?

6. What is Rosenblatt's attitude towards nature?

7. Is this clearly a descriptive essay? What does Rosenblatt describe?

8. Does Rosenblatt confine himself to fact in his descriptions? If not, is this a desirable method? a justifiable one?

9. Rosenblatt writes, "If the man in the water gave a lifeline to the people gasping for survival, he was likewise giving a lifeline to those who observed him." Is this a reasonable assessment of the man's action or mere hyperbole?

10. Evaluate the last sentence of Rosenblatt's essay. What does he mean? Does this conclusion logically follow from the rest of the essay?

Answers to Questions

1. The thesis, which is implied, is that we see in such heroic acts a confirmation of the best of human activity, that the man in the water represents "the possibility" in all of us.

2. Journalists writing news pieces ideally attempt to be objective—to focus on and simply report the facts. In this piece, Rosenblatt attempts to go beyond the details of the facts into the realm of philosophical speculation.

3. It provides a transition from the factual to the speculative. It establishes the scope of the essay and introduces the main ideas.

4. Among other things, it adds to the mystery of the nameless hero and allows the author to speculate on the reasons for the man's actions. The others are able to say, however modestly, why they did what they did. In contrast, we can only imagine why this individual sacrificed his life to save his fellow passengers. This essay might be contrasted with Gansberg's, p. 575.

5. See paragraph 8.

6. See paragraph 7. His position is essentially that of the American literary Naturalists. He presents nature as an indifferent, uncaring force.

7. There are descriptions in the essay, but one could argue that they are subordinate to the philosophical material. In fact, the descriptive information came to

Rosenblatt secondhand; he records the descriptions given by those who were on the scene. For example, his physical description of the man in the water comes from these sources. This does not lessen his achievement, of course.

8. In many passages Rosenblatt goes beyond the facts to record what can only be "fiction." He cannot, for example, know what the man in the water felt and thought, but he attempts to describe it in paragraph 6. In nonfiction, particularly reporting, this is not a desirable tactic. Given the substance and purpose of Rosenblatt's article, however, the method seems to work effectively here.

9. The sentiment may be exaggerated, but it is probably defensible. Many such examples of courage, survival, tragedy, etc., occur daily, yet a few somehow manage to capture the public's imagination.

10. Some would probably argue that humans can do better. But his point, given the scope of the essay, is valid.

Vocabulary
1. aesthetic (1)—pertaining to the beautiful or artistic

2. implacable (9)—incapable of being appeased

CHAPTER 28: NARRATION
P. 575

"38 WHO SAW MURDER DIDN'T CALL THE POLICE"—P. 575

Questions on Content, Structure, and Style

1. Does Gansberg's article have a thesis? What is it?

2. What point of view does Gansberg use? Who tells the story? What advantages and/or limitations does his narrative choice present?

3. In some ways Gansberg's article is a factual newspaper account of the Genovese incident; in other ways it seems more like fiction. Explain his technique.

4. Evaluate Gansberg's tone in this essay. What seems to be his attitude towards his subject?

5. Note the modifiers—especially the adverbs—that Gansberg uses when he records the statements of the witnesses. What does his choice of words reveal about these people?

6. What, apparently, were Gansberg's main sources for the facts of the Genovese case?

7. How does Gansberg structure his essay? What organizational pattern does he employ?

8. Why does Gansberg include the two paragraphs about the arrest of the suspect? Is the information given here necessary to the point he's trying to make? Does it add to the story?

9. What effect does the material presented in paragraphs 11–16 have? How can Gansberg know these details? Is this a good tactic for writers of descriptive essays?

10. What reason might Gansberg have for including the information about the cost of the homes in the neighborhood where the incident occurred? Is this relevant? Why or why not?

Answers to Questions

1. Whether the article has a thesis in the usual sense of the word is debatable, but it certainly presents a point of view. The implied "thesis" is that the U.S. is a nation of individuals so fearful of "getting involved" that they will stand by and watch while their fellow beings are murdered.

2. He uses a third person, omniscient narrator. The author is absent from the piece; the nameless narrator is able to recount events that could realistically not be known by the author, except secondhand. However, he tells the story as though he were always present.

3. In part, Gansberg's piece is similar to the contemporary style of blending fact and fiction that some have called "faction." The story is based on fact, but Gansberg, rather than simply recording the facts, creates a short-story effect by the way he uses a narrator, records dialogue, etc.

4. Although the narrative "voice" offers no direct comment, it is clear from what is said that Gansberg is horrified by what happened and finds the incident symptomatic of a major social problem. He obviously feels compassion for Genovese and disdain for those who failed to help her.

5. He has people say things "sheepishly," "knowingly if quite casually," "without emotion." They shrug, peek out from behind partly closed doors—in short they seem every bit as uncaring and aloof as one might expect from the facts.

6. The police and Genovese's neighbors. Most likely, his story is based at least in part on earlier news accounts.

7. He begins in the present, then recounts the Genovese murder in chronological order, then he introduces the fact of the suspect's arrest and closes with the witnesses' comments.

8. From the standpoint of the Genovese story and the point Gansberg is making about what happened, the material is probably unnecessary. However, from a journalistic standpoint, the material is significant and it probably answers (as well as could be expected at the time) questions most readers would ask.

9. The details could have come in part from the witnesses' accounts, but much of it is certainly fictional—Gansberg's way of dramatizing the incident and stressing the horror the victim felt. One appalling side-note that instructors might point out regarding this horror felt by Genovese and other victims: in 1995 Genovese's murderer, Winston Mosely, stated to parole officials that he has suffered more than his victim because for her it was "a one-minute affair, but for the person who's caught, it's forever."

10. The facts and figures indicate that the neighborhood is upper-middle to middle-class (remember this is 1964) and composed primarily of single-family dwellings. Though Gansberg does not say so, the implication is clear: if it can happen here it can happen anywhere. These are presumably well-to-do, hard-working, successful people. Yet they failed to respond the way we might expect they should.

Vocabulary

1. recitation (4)—account, as if by rote

2. staid (6)—reserved, grave

3. distraught (26)—upset, worried

"THE TALKIES"—P. 578

Questions on Content, Structure, and Style

1. The first paragraph of this essay tells the reader what the writer is not going to write about. Why does Lileks begin this way?

2. Throughout the essay, Lileks uses dialogue—he repeats the words of the movie talkers. What does this add to the essay?

3. When does Lileks announce his distinct purpose in writing this essay?

4. What specific names and places does Lileks use to add reality to this essay?

5. To what senses of the reader does Lileks appeal as he retells his experience?

6. How does Lileks attempt to be fair in his condemnation of the talkers?

7. While entertainment is probably not the main purpose of this essay, Lileks maintains a humorous tone throughout. Why does he adopt this approach?

8. Which detail was most memorable and why?

9. This essay comes from *Notes of a Nervous Man*. What other public annoyances do you suppose make Lileks "nervous"?

10. What is a pet peeve of yours? Describe one specific time you encountered it.

Answers to Questions

1. Lileks uses these universal experiences so that the audience will identify with the movie-going experience and irritations generally associated with it. He is setting a tone of annoyance that the audience can identify with.

2. Repeating the exact dialogue of the talkers adds a sense of reality and helps the reader picture the incident more clearly.

3. In paragraph 23, Lileks tells moviegoers to think before they talk long and continually through a movie, spoiling the experience for the rest of the audience.

4. Using names such as Siskel and Ebert, Dots, Curious George, Gene Hackman, and Willem Defoe validates the narrative and the reader can experience its details with the writer.

5. In paragraph 1, Lileks appeals to sight, sound, touch, and taste. The rest of the details are primarily sight and sound.

6. Lileks tries to be reasonable by stating, in paragraph 3, that he can understand a whispered or limited comment; it is the loud and persistent comments that he is protesting.

7. The humorous tone may take enough edge off his anger that readers can identify themselves in the essay and respond positively. Also, readers who are not the talkers can enjoy the essay more and can laugh along with Lileks since they have probably had similar experiences.

8. Student responses will vary; however, most can point to a specific detail that stuck in their minds.

9. Although there are many other public annoyances that probably would bother Lileks, students might pick up on paragraph 17, where Lileks indicates he is a smoker and his behavior might bother others as much as talkers bother him!

10. Students will have different pet peeves to discuss.

Vocabulary

1. decibels (3)—units for measuring sound

2. empirical (5)—based on numerous experiences

3. epiphany (5)—a moment of sudden understanding

4. malicious (7)—with mean intentions

5. nostalgic (7)—causing a longing for something long ago

6. telekinesis (18)—the movement of an object caused while not in contact with the body generating the force: "mind over matter"

7. sodium pentothal (21)—a truth drug

8. mole (21)—a dark-colored, raised spot or mark on the skin

"BEAUTY: WHEN THE OTHER DANCER IS THE SELF"—*P. 581*
Questions on Content, Structure, and Style

1. What is the significance of Walker's title? What does it mean?

2. What point of view does Walker use in this essay? Who is the narrator?

3. What verb tense is this essay written in? Where, in time, does the author "stand" in relation to the events she is describing? How does this relate to her method of organization?

4. In several instances Walker uses italics. Why? How do these passages differ from the others?

5. Why, in the first few episodes she recounts, does Walker place so much emphasis on clothing—what she wore, what people thought of her garments, etc.?

6. How does the scar change the narrator? How does this relate to the thesis, or main point, of the essay?

7. Why does Walker include the poem "On Sight" in her essay? How does it contribute to the meaning of her essay?

8. What does Walker's daughter see in the blind eye? How does this change the author's perception of her scar? herself?

9. Evaluate the final paragraph. Is this an effective conclusion? Why or why not?

10. This is obviously a personal essay, one that records a specific problem in the life of one individual. Is it more than that? Does the general theme of Walker's essay have universal application?

Answers to Questions

1. The title refers to her metaphorical quest—in the essay—for the meaning of beauty. It also refers to the incident (and the idea) related in the final paragraph. She has come to terms with her past, her other self.

2. She uses the first person. Obviously, she is writing a personal experience essay, but it might be pointed out to students that a first person narrative does not always mean that the author and the narrator are the same person.

3. She is reflecting on past events, but she uses the present tense. This underscores the reflective nature of the essay. Notice that she uses age as a focal point for each episode and that the organization is chronological.

4. The italic passages represent the voice of the narrator in the present. Because past episodes are related in present tense as well, the italics serve to distinguish between past and present, between the old and new "self." Too, they function as transitional devices.

5. This stresses the difference between superficial, or external, beauty, and the deeper beauty she comes to discover within herself.

6. The scar changes the nature of the girl completely—or, at least, she thinks so. She has not fundamentally changed, but because she has been so aware of external beauty—her clothes, her appearance, her actions—she feels who she is has been radically altered. The wound makes her "blind" in more ways than one.

7. This passage is pivotal to the essay. Suddenly recalling—and confronting—the words of the doctor about the possibility of losing sight in both eyes, Walker learns, for the first time, to really see. The desert is bleak, not of interest to most people, who would say it is all the same, monotonous. Walker learns that the desert has beauty. She looks past the "flags" of vision—the symbols—and really sees. This passage provides transition from one state and time to another.

8. The child sees an image that resembles the picture of the earth taken from the moon that appears on "Big Blue Marble." Walker has to this point been uneasy about her daughter looking at the scarred eye. When she asks, "Mommy, where did you get that world in your eye?" the pain—most of it anyway—left.

9. The conclusion is highly effective. It relates to the title (see question 1 above) and brings the essay full circle. The final episode is a resolution of the conflict within herself that the author recounts.

10. The essay has universal application, as most effective personal experience essays do. Readers will not have the same specific problem, but they may have some problem that creates self-doubt and dissatisfaction.

Vocabulary
1. crinolines (4)—billowing underskirts made from a stiff, starched fabric

2. boisterous (16)—rowdy

CHAPTER 29: ESSAYS FOR FURTHER ANALYSIS: MULTIPLE STRATEGIES AND STYLES
P. 589

"I Have a Dream"—P. 589
Questions on Content, Structure, and Style

1. King's "I Have a Dream" is a speech rather than an essay. What stylistic tactics does he use that seem especially effective for oral presentation?

2. Considering King's audience, what might be the main purpose of his speech? Is his intent to be persuasive?

3. Analyze King's opening sentence. Why is it appropriate?

4. What extended analogy does King use when discussing the Constitution and the Declaration. Is the metaphor a good one?

5. One rhetorical tactic that King employs especially well is repetition. Give two examples of his use of this device.

6. What is the effect of repetition generally? in King's speech?

7. King is noted for his belief in both racial harmony and nonviolent protest. Does this speech reflect that belief?

8. King quotes from both the Declaration of Independence and the song "America." What effect does this have on his message?

9. What word (and its variants) is used most often in this speech? Why is it important?

10. Is King's argument logical or emotional? Does he appeal to our minds or our hearts?

Answers to Questions

1. The most obvious device is repetition. It should be noted as well that his language is rhythmical and simple, and his sentences short—terse and emphatic.

2. King's primary audience shared his beliefs. In this sense, the speech may be seen more as an inspirational message than persuasive discourse.

3. The "Five score years ago" echoes the beginning of Lincoln's Emancipation Speech. The "great American" is Lincoln, and King is standing in the shadow of the Lincoln Memorial. The speech was given at a massive protest march celebrating the Emancipation Proclamation.

4. He compares the two documents to a check. His analogy is both appropriate and consistent.

5. See paragraphs 2, 4, 11–18, 20–27.

6. Repetition is used for emphasis. In speeches it works especially well because of the limitations placed on the audience. Readers are able to follow points much more easily, for example, and can reread if necessary. King, in this speech, frequently uses extended passages in which he employs repetition—for example, the repeated phrase "I have a dream." This not only underscores his point, but also contrasts with the reality he describes.

7. Yes. See paragraphs 6 and 7.

8. The quotes, which reflect the American ideal, offer a contrast to the American reality. King's dream is only to have that reality fulfilled. By citing lines that Americans know well and believe in, he emphasizes the point that Blacks only want the rights held dear by all Americans.

9. The word is "free" (or the variant "freedom"). Freedom, of course, is the subject both of the speech and of King's "dream." Again, this speech was delivered at a celebration of the Emancipation Proclamation, which freed slaves in America.

10. Though the ideas presented are grounded in logic, the overall tone of the speech is emotional.

Vocabulary
1. languishing (2)—without energy or spirit, weak

2. inextricably (6)—tangled, too complex to unravel

"POLITICS AND THE ENGLISH LANGUAGE"—P. 593
Questions on Content, Structure, and Style
1. Summarize Orwell's claim.

2. What proof does Orwell offer to support his position? Why are the five quoted excerpts important to his argument?

3. What cause-and-effect cycle does Orwell describe in paragraph 2? Why does he include the line about the "man who may take to drink"?

4. In your own words, describe what Orwell means by "dying metaphors," "operators or verbal false limbs," "pretentious diction," and "meaningless words."

5. Describe Orwell's tone.

6. Describe the type of reader who would be most receptive to Orwell's argument.

7. Review Orwell's six rules for improved writing. Which rule do you most often break? Explain.

8. Do you agree with Orwell's claim that writers use euphemisms as a way to express truths we would rather not face? List a few such euphemisms that you are aware of, from either current/past events or our daily lives.

9. Reread Orwell's conclusion. What is he asking of his readers?

10. Choose an excerpt from any piece of published writing (a newspaper or magazine, a textbook) and explain how it violates one or more of Orwell's rules for effective writing.

Answers to Questions

1. Orwell claims that the English language is in a state of deplorable, but reversible, decay; a return to clear thinking—necessary for clear, effective writing—is necessary.

2. Orwell discusses several trends in modern writing that he believes indicate muddled or lazy thinking, and as proof/illustration of these ills he offers five excerpts from various writings. He assesses each of these excerpts to reveal specific weaknesses in contemporary writing and thought processes, often contrasting these pieces to the more effective prose style of earlier times.

3. According to Orwell, an effect can become a cause which reinforces the original cause and intensifies its effect; accordingly, language decays because our thoughts have become "foolish," but our thoughts are foolish because our language has decayed. He uses the analogy (one that instructors might note is not hackneyed or worn out, as are the "dying metaphors" Orwell later derides) to illustrate his point.

4. "Dying metaphors" are those metaphors so worn and stale that they fail to create a real image or meaning in the mind of the reader or writer; "operators or verbal

false limbs" are phrases that replace more meaningful simple verb constructions in an attempt to make the mundane seem profound; "pretentious diction" includes words used to glorify "simple statements" but which actually decrease precision and clarity.

5. Orwell's tone is one of reason and concern as he discusses the abuses of English and seeks to convince his reader that this decay can and must be stopped.

6. This essay was originally published in Shooting an Elephant and Other Essays and as part of this collection was intended for educated readers who are interested in writing, language, and thought. He seems to be speaking particularly to those readers who are in a position to wage an active campaign against "slovenliness" in writing and thought—teachers, writers, or journalists, perhaps, to name a few.

7. Students' responses will vary but should indicate an awareness of their own writing processes.

8. Some examples students might cite include the many euphemisms surrounding death (for example, "passed away" instead of "died.") Instructors might refer students to Mitford's "To Bid the World Farewell" for an in-depth examination of euphemism in the English language. Other examples might come from current events (for example, the "ethnic cleansing" in the former Yugoslavia instead of "killing people of different ethnic backgrounds") or economic trends ("corporate downsizing" instead of "firing employees").

9. Orwell asks his readers to improve their own verbal English use, as a start, and perhaps then take the next step to "jeer loudly enough" to perhaps bring about the end of "some worn-out and useless phrase."

10. Student responses to this question will vary and should result in interesting class discussions of the ineffective prose Orwell decries.

Vocabulary
1. decadent (1)—ruined, depraved

2. archaism (1)—something outdated, obsolete

3. slovenliness (2)—disorder

4. hackneyed (4)—trite, overused

5. metaphor (5)—figurative language

6. evocative (5)—causing feelings

7. banal (6)—common

8. profundity (7)—depth, significance

9. sordid (7)—self-serving, foul

10. jargon (7)—meaningless language, gibberish

11. parody (10)—copy, imitation

12. gross (10)—crass, coarse

13. superfluous (I 1)—unnecessary, excessive

14. dustbin (19)— British term for trash can

"A MODEST PROPOSAL"—P. 604
Questions on Content, Structure, and Style
1. What is Swift's "modest proposal"?

2. Describe Swift's writing voice.

3. Define satire, consulting a dictionary if necessary.

4. What is Swift's purpose in writing? What emotional impact does he want his essay to have on his readers?

5. Reread paragraph 12. In what way have the landlords "already devoured" the parents of children born into poverty?

6. What is particularly ironic about Swift's suggestion that "infants' flesh" is especially appropriate to serve at weddings and christenings (paragraph 28)?

7. In paragraph 29 Swift lists several solutions to the problems of poverty but indicates that these will not work because they will not be "put . . . in[to] practice." What does he reveal about human nature by implying that people would rather consume the children of the poor than give these other solutions a chance to work?

8. Review paragraph 32, Swift's address of those who might oppose his "modest proposal." What is he actually saying about the plight of the poor?

9. Why is Swift's use of satire likely more effective than a straightforward plea for help for Ireland's poor?

10. What topics are effective subjects for satire? List a few events or situations—either current or historical—that could be the focus of a Swift-like satire.

Answers to Questions

1. Swift's modest proposal is that the children of the Irish poor should be sold as food for the British upper classes' consumption.

2. On the surface, Swift's voice seems to be one of sincere concern, a writer who has calmly assessed the situation and is presenting a rational solution.

3. Satire exposes human vice and holds it up for ridicule, often through irony and sarcasm. Swift's essay is considered a masterpiece of satire as he reveals the cruel injustices of eighteenth-century British society.

4. Swift intends to outrage his reading audience, stirring them to consider the true plight of the poor and hopefully take action toward a genuine solution to the tragedy.

5. The landlords "devour" the parents figuratively by stripping them of any individual rights and freedoms that might allow them to prosper, and by using the labor of the poor to sustain the wealth of the upper classes.

6. This is particularly ironic because weddings and christenings are celebrations of life and the promise of new generations, a promise that is completely broken by the consumption of a society's children.

7. The solutions he mentions and then discards—taxes and increased use of domestic labor, social prudence rather than luxurious excess, heightened awareness of social responsibility toward others, and honesty in business dealings—are all reasonable, potential solutions to poverty, but they all come with a price: sacrifice and self-discipline. Swift implies that it is far easier for self-absorbed, lazy people to continue to consume (eat children) than it is to sacrifice.

8. He implies that the state of the poor is so wretched and brutal that many would, in fact, have suffered less had they not lived past infancy.

9. Satire allows Swift to reach readers who might not be receptive to a more traditional form of argument (a wealthy reader, perhaps, who is tired of hearing about the poor and feels that it is neither his concern nor responsibility). Through satire, he exposes the complacency that allows the privileged and educated—his readers, in fact—to ignore poverty.

10. Student answers to this question will vary; instructors might note that politics has long been a favorite subject for satire.

Vocabulary
1. importuning (1)—asking

2. alms (1)—money or food for the poor

3. prodigious (2)—enormous

4. dam (4)—mother, usually used in reference to animals

5. raiment (4)—clothing

6. hitherto (6)—until now

7. glutted (13)—flooded

8. repine (14)—to feel dejected

9. refinement (17)—alteration

10. censure (17)—condemn

11. desponding (19)—despairing

12. vintners (25)—wine makers

13. emulation (26)—rivalry

14. enumerated (27)—counted

"THE GREAT PERSON-HOLE COVER DEBATE: A MODEST PROPOSAL"—P. 611
Questions on Content, Structure, and Style
1. What is the "debate" Van Gelder describes? Is her personal example at the beginning a good way to introduce this debate? Why or why not?

2. Why does the author quote so heavily from the booklet on fish and game laws?

3. In paragraph 11, Van Gelder uses comparison when she points out progress being made in eliminating racially-loaded language. Is the analogy effective?

4. What opposition parties does Van Gelder identify? What are the reasons for their resistance to non-biased language?

5. Who are the most dangerous of those opposed to such language change? Why?

6. Why does Van Gelder use the term "woman-handling" in paragraph 7?

7. What is the author's proposal? Does she want her proposal to be enacted? Why does she make the proposal?

8. Who is Van Gelder addressing in the conclusion? Who are the "fellas"? Do you think they will be convinced by her argument? Why? Why not?

9. The title is an allusion to Jonathan Swift's essay, "A Modest Proposal," printed immediately previously to this essay. Read Swift's proposal. How are the two arguments structured similarly? How are they different?

10. Think of a situation or practice you believe needs examining— e.g., large lecture classes, obsessive television watching, internet regulation. Write an essay that might be published as a letter to the editor in which you "solve" the problem with a "proposal" which satirically clarifies your stance.

Answers to Questions

1. The debate is over the use of non-sexist language. Van Gelder's personal example is a fitting opening because it illustrates the feelings many women have when confronted with gender-specific language that doesn't include them. Also, the example shows the attitude Van Gelder is most concerned with: the belief that using male-oriented terms to refer to either/both genders is simply a convenient tradition.

2. Had the author just described the booklet's language in her own terms, the extent and character of the offensive language would not have been so strongly established. Also, quoting the pamphlet keeps a reader from any possible thought that she was misinterpreting the words or being over-sensitive and whiny; the words speak for themselves.

3. The "flesh-colored" band-aid analogy is helpful because it shows that the same argument of tradition ("old-time's sake") and convenience would never be accepted in a realm other than gender— race, in this instance. Often it is easiest to see the problem with an argument when that argument is applied to other similar circumstances to check its validity.

4. Van Gelder identifies one group that dislikes gender-neutral language because they believe it is put forward by extreme feminists and it will corrupt both traditional language and the pleasant distinctions between the sexes. The other objectors are those who believe the issue of gender-bias in language is "trivial," that it is not an issue worthy of concern or redress.

5. Those who think the issue is trivial are more dangerous because they are well-intended and believe they are being open-minded and fair about gender discrimination. It is this sort of acceptance and being taken for granted that has kept gender bias in language alive so long.

6. By replacing "man" with "woman" in this word, Van Gelder draws attention to the prevalence of such gender-loaded expressions while sarcastically referring to the suspected abuse (man-handling) of language by feminists.

7. The author proposes we replace male-oriented language with female language if simplicity is such an important issue (paragraph 13) since it is only "only fair to give 'she' a turn." Although she doesn't intend this proposal to be implemented, her discussion shows how unacceptable such gender-bias would be for men if the situation were reversed.

8. The "fellas" are the Vermont Fish and Game Commissioner and others of a similar mind. They might not be convinced by this argument and it's sometimes caustic tone, but then they are fairly set in their opinion already. However, others who are undecided on the issue might be convinced by the author's examples of ubiquitous male-oriented language and the strong hypothetical examples in her proposal.

9. The essays have a parallel structure. They both begin by describing the problems, and then they give proposals for solutions. Both essays end with thoughts about the effects of their proposals, but Swift details those effects whereas Van Gelder just compels us to imagine how men would react to reversed gender-bias in language. Swift maintains a tone of mock seriousness throughout while Van Gelder explains her points in a straightforward argumentative style at several points (paragraphs 8-12 in particular).

10. Student responses will vary.

Vocabulary

1. forthright (5)—straightforward, direct

2. Newspeak (6)—the use of misleading talk to form public opinion

3. consternation (7)—amazement, confused wonder

4. vive la difference (7)—a French term of acclaim, "Long live the difference!"

5. misogynists (8)—people who hate women

6. jeopardizing (9)—putting at risk

CHAPTER 30: LITERATURE
P. 613

"WE REAL COOL"—P. 613

Questions on Content, Structure, and Style

1. What is the narrators' point of view in this poem? Why has Brooks made this choice?

2. Characterize the pool players from the sense Brooks gives in the first seven lines. How does she achieve this impression so quickly?

3. Why did Brooks include the second line, "Seven at the Golden Shovel," in the title?

4. How does the word choice add to the picture the poet is drawing of these young men?

5. How does the rhythm of the poem relate to the content?

6. Describe the rhyme pattern of the poem.

7. Why do all the lines end with "We" instead of ending at the periods?

8. What is the effect of the last line? Why does the line mean more coming from the players themselves?

9. This poem was written before 1960. Does it have relevance today? What parallels are there in our current society?

10. All of us belong to several different groups: families, professional groups, social cliques, school companions or classmates, ethnic groups, etc. List the groups of which you are a part. What type of language characterizes each group? What are specific phrases you would use when interacting with each of the groups? Write a first person poem or short narrative that demonstrates the nature of one of the groups by emphasizing this specific language.

Answers to Questions

1. Many principles hold true for poetry as well as prose; writers who show their subjects to the reader create more impact. When the reader hears these "cool" pool players speak for themselves, they become more real than if described from a third person point of view.

2. These young men are school dropouts who appear in the first seven lines to be boasting about their tough, "cool" lifestyle. Brooks achieves this effect so quickly

by selecting her images judiciously, condensing the images to the essence of the players' behavior, and by mimicking their dialect.

3. The specificity of the location and name of the pool "joint" adds a feeling of authenticity to the poem. The word "golden" in the title is ironic since the ultimate sum of these players' lives is not very golden.

4. The very sound of the language—the short, clipped sentences, the rhyme and repetition—create the rhythm of an identifiable dialect. The style of the language also suggests "jive talk," an earlier style of rhythmic speech reminiscent of today's "rap" style.

5. The rhyme pattern is best described by looking at the words immediately before the periods, not the exact last word as would be more typical. The pattern is aab-bccdd.

6. By putting the "We" at the end of the lines, the focus on the pool players themselves—the first person point of view—is emphasized and the rhythm changes dramatically. Students will see, by reading the poem aloud, that the simple rhyme scheme is far less "sing song" when the words are arranged this way. They will also notice how the narrators's voices—we—automatically dominate in this arrangement.

7. The repetitive cadence sets up a pattern that seems to gain speed until abruptly stopped by the strong last blunt statement. The rhythm mimics the rhythm of these young men's lives— fast, rapid-fire, and "grooving," with a dramatic, fated ending.

8. The last three words bring the reader up short after the rhythm and arrogance of the previous lines. Brooks's abrupt and contrasting conclusion mirrors the lives these young men may live; while they probably will take pride in their tough lives, they are at the same time aware that death is imminent and certain for them. The impact of this statement is stronger on the reader since it comes from the men themselves and is an accepted part of their vision of their future. Students might have a discussion of whether the pool players are bragging about this fate, or lamenting it.

9. Students should easily see a parallel between Brooks's pool players and today's gang members. "We sing sin," makes a particularly close comparison to gangster rap and the pride in negative behavior can be seen in gang values, initiation rites, and boastful demeanor. Also, the life expectation rate for young ghetto residents is appallingly low, leading to the same kind of dismal future vision for today's young "pool players."

10. Student responses will vary.

"Those Winter Sundays"—P. 614
Questions on Content, Structure, and Style

1. Who is the narrator of the poem? How has his perspective on his father's actions changed since he was a young boy?

2. What early morning activity of his father does the narrator remember now? What does the reader learn from the detailed description of the father's hands?

3. What was the son's attitude as a child toward his father? How did he relate to his father? What was the father's attitude toward the boy? What evidence do you see that the father cared for his family despite the harshness of their life?

4. Focus in prose is essential; it is the essence of poetry. For the narrator, growing up was full of negative and positive experiences. What does the focus on these two small moments say about the poet's intent? Why not tell more of the story?

5. What do the concluding lines reveal about the poet's mature perspective?

6. Where does Hayden use alliteration in this poem?

7. What descriptive words rely heavily on sensory images?

8. Describe the rhyme scheme and rhythm pattern of this poem.

9. Read "Sister Flowers" by Maya Angelou, p. 342 in this text. In both Angelou's narrative and Hayden's poem, the authors look back on experiences in their youth with an adult perspective. If Hayden were to write this poem in a prose narrative style similar to Angelou's, what more would he include? Would he include a comment such as in lines 13 and 14? If Angelou were to write a poem called "Sister Flowers," what two images should she focus on to reveal her mature perspective on Sister Flowers's influence? What would be lost in doing so? What would be gained?

10. What single moment capsulizes the attitude and or behavior of one of your parents when you were young? One of your siblings? One of your best friends? One of your most important teachers? How do you see that moment differently now? Write a poem or a narrative or descriptive passage focusing on that moment and your change in perspective.

Answers to Questions

1. An adult child of the father is the narrator. The speaker is probably middle-aged or older since he can now reflect on his father's actions with more appreciation. He probably has experienced many of the same family responsibilities which go unnoticed and unappreciated, so now he can relate to the "austere and lonely" obligations his father fulfilled.

2. Every morning the father would have to stoke the fire to warm the house before the rest of the family arose. His hands were cracked from working outside in harsh weather.

3. The son obeyed his father to avoid his anger and paid little attention to him. The sons fear of the "chronic angers" might have been a young boy's reaction to the father's weariness and constant working. Although the father may have displayed ill-humor from the burden of his responsibilities, there is evidence of a contrasting tender caring for the family, particularly in the polishing of his son's shoes. As an adult, the son interprets his father's actions far differently than he did as a child.

4. Focusing on these two incidents of kindness—stoking the fires and polishing the shoes—clearly establishes the essence of the father that only a mature son can appreciate. The incidents went unnoticed by a young boy; the responsibility of caring for a family that equates, for Hayden, to love is crystalized in these two specific moments. The details of the poet's home life are not really important in this poem. The focus is on changed perspective through maturity. Making a carefully chosen fragment of experience speak for a concept is the process of poetry.

5. The last two lines show a certain regret the son now has that he could not see the love in his father's actions.

6. Lines 4 and 5: "weekday weather" and "banked fires blaze"

7. Line 2: "blueblack cold," sense of touch and sight

   Line 3: "cracked hands that ached," sense of touch and sight

   Line 6: "hear the cold splintering, breaking," sense of hearing

8. The poem contains three, free verse stanzas.

9. Student responses will vary.

10. Student responses will vary.

Vocabulary
   1. chronic (9)—occurring repeatedly

   2. austere (14)—harsh, severe

"A MYSTERY OF HEROISM"—P. 614
Questions on Content, Structure, and Style
   1. Why does Collins initially decide to make his dangerous run? How does that motivation change throughout the story?

2. Does Collins believe he is a hero? What thoughts go through his mind about the courage of his act?

3. What is the attitude of Collins's peers toward his mission (for example, see paragraphs 39 and 40)?

4. What figures of speech does Crane use to describe Collins's terror when he arrives at the well?

5. How do Collins's thoughts and actions contrast to those of others on the battlefield? Why is this contrast important?

6. Cite some examples of the sensory detail Crane uses to create an atmospheric background for Collins's actions

7. What is your opinion of Collins's actions? Are they truly heroic? Are they foolhardy? Is noble intention a necessary aspect of heroism?

8. What is the significance of the spilled bucket at the end of the story?

9. Collins believes that he is an "intruder in the land of fine deeds." He had been, as a child, "irritable, childish, diabolical." He was not, in his estimation, a shameless, guiltless character capable of noble efforts. Is there a difference between heroism and heroic acts? Is general character a necessary component of either?

10. Read "The Heroes Among Us," page 519 in this text. How does Wolf define heroism? Would Collins fall into Wolf's category of celebrity, hero, or neither? Would Crane agree with this definition?

Answers to Questions

1. At the beginning, Collins makes an idle comment to his compatriots, thinking out loud how good it would be to have a drink of water. As the story progresses, the trip to the well becomes almost a game of "chicken." His companions may have "forced him into this affair," but he later takes on the errand as his own blind quest.

2. Collins wavers about his heroism. He recognizes his dazed and "supernaturally strange" state as the unthinking determination heroes have in pursuit of their goal. At the same time, he questions whether or not he can truly be heroic because he, in fact, has committed petty, negative acts in his life. Heroes have "no shames in their lives." He is not really sure how this "dramatically great" moment in his life can be categorized.

3. Collins's peers are surprised—even dumbfounded—at his undertaking. They teased him and intimidated him into action, but are astonished that he is actually

following through. In paragraphs 39 and 40, they treat him as a celebrity, giving him more attention that he has ever had from them before. Whereas his comrades earlier made fun of him for even contemplating such a bold action, they have a curious fascination with him as he starts out.

4. Crane uses similes and metaphors to characterize Collins's fear. The sky was "full of fiends," a "grasp of claws" tears at his heart, and he reacts to a loud and colorful explosion reflected in the well as a man would "in withdrawing his head from a furnace."

5. The first half of the narrative is dominated by images of men committed to dangerous acts for important strategic and political goals. Two privates were even discussing "the greatest questions of the national existence" during all the chaos (paragraph 5). The seriousness of purpose and the carnage of the battle is in stark contrast to the triviality of Collins's concern for a drink of water.

6. Crane uses extremely rich visual, touch, smell, and auditory, imagery. A few vivid examples are noted below.

Paragraph 3: "A glittering bugle swung clear of the rider's back as fell headlong the horse and the man. In the air was an odor as from a conflagration."

Paragraph 5: "From beyond a curtain of green woods there came the sound of some stupendous scuffle, as if. . ."

Paragraph 7: ". . . a falsetto shriek"

Paragraph 14: ". . . a noise which resembled the flapping of shutters during a wild gale of winter."

Paragraph 15: ". . . white legs stretched horizontally on the ground."

Paragraph 60: "As he ran the canteens knocked together with a rhythmical tinkling."

Paragraph 61: ". . . hootings, yells, howls."

Paragraph 69: ". . . long blue line of the regiment. . ." "He was aware of some deep wheel-ruts and hoofprints in the sod beneath his feet."

7. Crane has given a reader enough clues to support different arguments about Collins's heroism. The heart of the question is whether a hero can be "blindly . . . led by quaint emotions," or whether purpose and motivation are part of the definition of heroism. Collins acts out of fear ("He was mad from the threats of destruction") and out of a certain machismo. Student arguments will be around whether heroism is a product or a process.

8. The fact that the water is spilled and, therefore, Collins's mission seems even

more pointless can be used to argue that Crane does not believe Collins is heroic but that his actions were empty and meaningless. A larger question is whether this emptiness and Collins's "heroism" suggest a futility to other actions in war.

9. Student responses will vary.

10. Student responses will vary.

Vocabulary

1. caissons (1)—two-wheeled wagons for carrying ammunition

2. redoubled (6)—made twice as great

3. demeanors (6)—outward behaviors, manners

4. stolidity (6)—dullness

5. falsetto (7)—artificial way of singing higher than normal

6. grapple (9)—to grip and hold

7. imprecation (12)—curse

8. ruck (14)—a heap or stack

9. ominous (23)—having an evil character

10. jeers (23)—rude, sarcastic remarks

12. pious (30)—having religious devotion

13. gesticulating (38)—moving body or limbs energetically to express one's meaning

14. quaint (51)—whimsical

16. retraction (52)—withdrawal of a statement

17. diabolical (56)—devilish, wicked

18. furtive (63)—hidden, sly

19. indolent (63)—slow, sluggish

20. derided (65)—laughed at, made fun of

21. skylarking (81)—playful, frolicsome